This book is dedicated to
the Greek Alpine Club of Athens
on its 50th anniversary

G. SFIKAS

The mountains
of
Greece

By GEORGE SFIKAS

Maps and sketches are by the author,
as are all the photographs, unless
otherwise acknowledged

ATHENS

ISBN 960 226 067 X

Reprinted 1990

Distributed by:
EFSTATHIADIS GROUP S.A.
Ag. Athanasiou Str. GR. 145 65 Anixi Attikis Tel. 8136871-2
14 Valtetsiou St. GR 106 80 Athens Tel. 3615011
34 Olympou-Diikitiriou St. GR. 546 30 Thessaloniki Tel. 511781

EFSTATHIADIS GROUP
Bookshop: 84, Academias St. Tel. 3637439

LIST OF CONTENTS

Part I: GENERAL BACKGROUND INFORMATION

Part II: THE MOUNTAINS

Part III: REFERENCE SECTION

"To live in plenty is not the same as to live well. Living well requires that one feels in harmony with nature, that one knows what to look for: how to find happiness in simple things, in the view of a mountain or the sea, in a beautiful day, in the company of family or friends" (transl.)

William Fulbright

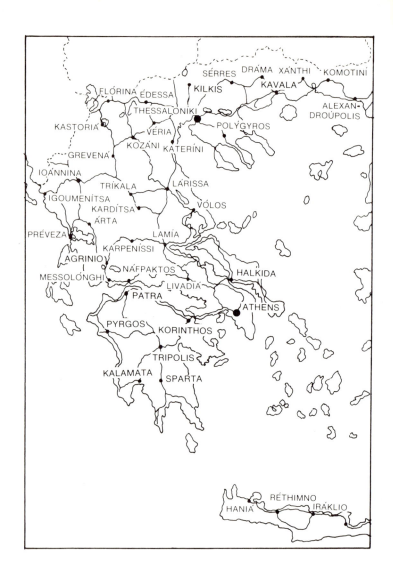

Greece: map of major towns and roads

Part I

GENERAL BACKGROUND INFORMATION

INTRODUCTION

Greece is known throughout the world as the land of sun and sea. A child of the sea. Greece is cradled by the tranquil Mediterranean, with hundreds of islands large and small in attendance. It is also the child of the sun, and can point to one of the highest sunshine records in Europe. But most of all, with four-fifths of its surface high above sea level, Greece is a country of mountains *par excellence.*

The Greek peninsula is basically a chain of mountains which extends like a wedge towards the Mediterranean in the south. There are few countries where high mountains are to be found so close to the sea. The best-known of Greece's peaks—Mt Ólympos, with 2,917 m elevation-is not the country's only high mountain. There are many others over 2,500 m high, and even more exceeding 2,000 m, ready to afford the greatest pleasure to mountaineers and nature-lovers alike.

In general, the best season for climbing the Greek mountains is from April to June, when the weather is likely to be dry and sunny without it having become too hot as yet. At this time of year there is still snow on the higher summits, while at the less extreme elevations there is a delightful profusion of lovely highland wild flowers.

Further climbing expeditions can be made during the summer, up such famous peaks as Mt Ólympos, Mt Ghióna, Mt Gamíla, and others. This is also the season for the longer climbs in the Pindus range or the Macedonian mountains which require more than one day.

There are winter sports centres for skiing on Mt Parnassós, Mt Veloúhi, Mt Pílion, Mt Vérmion and elsewhere, which can also serve as the points of departure for the more difficult winter ascents by walkers as well as rock climbers.

THE BIRTH OF THE GREEK MOUNTAINS

In the millions of years that have elapsed since the earth turned from a liquid fiery mass into a solid body, its surface crust has undergone vast upheavals and its morphology has changed time and time again. As the fireball cooled more and more, its outer crust puckered and shrank, and this wrinkling gradually resulted in the formation of great mountain ranges.

This process of the growth of new mountain is known as orogenesis. The most recent such on our planet was the so-called Alpine orogenesis, which began at the end of the Mesozoic period and reached its climax during the Caenozoic, and essentially continues even today. This was the time when the big mountain ranges were formed which we are familiar with in our own time: the European Alps, the Jura mountains, the Appenines, the Carpathians, the Transylvanian and the Dinaric Alps, as well as the various Greek mountain ranges.

Originally, the land which is today the Greek peninsula and Asia Minor lay at the bottom of the large ocean known to geologists as Tithis. The huge upward pressures which gradually raised the floor of this ocean kept thrusting upward until the large landmass which contains today's Greece and West Asia Minor had been pushed well above sea level. Subsequently, as the result of further pressures and consequent shifts in land masses, a part of this land, known as Aeghis, subsided again and became the Aegean sea. Further to the west of it the upthrust continued, forming what is now the Greek peninsula and the Greek mountains. In this way, fossil rocks which aeons ago were formed in the depths of the Tithis ocean have been thrust to great heights above sea level and are to be found today on the summits of the Greek mountains.

MORPHOLOGY

The Greek mountains are a continuation of the Dinaric Alps in Yugoslavia, which in their turn are an offshoot of the Alps proper. The Dinaric Alps give their name to the Dinarian Arc of which they form the beginning, and which continues southwards through the Greek mainland and via the islands of Kýthira and Antikýthira to Crete. Here it takes a more easterly turn, forming the mountain chain across Crete, and continues via Kárpathos and Rhodes to end in the Taurus range in Turkey's Southern Anatolia.

On Greek territory, the main line of this arc includes the Pindus range in the north of the country, and the mountains of Central Greece, the Peloponnese, Crete, Kárpathos and Rhodes. There are also a number of smaller ranges which are offshoots of this master chain. One of these faces east and forms a mountain highland wall at the northern borders of Greece with the peaks of Mt Varnoús, Mt Kaïmaktsalán, Mt Órvilos, Mt Béles, Mt Phalakrón of Drama, and ending in the Rhodópi range.

Another of these offshoot ranges starts from the Northern Pindus and runs south-east via Mt Kamvoúnia, Mt Piéria, Mt Ólympos, Káto Ólympos, Mt Kíssavos, Mt Pílion, Mt Óthrys and the mountains of Euboea.

Rock formations

The main rock to be met with in the Greek mountains is limestone in its

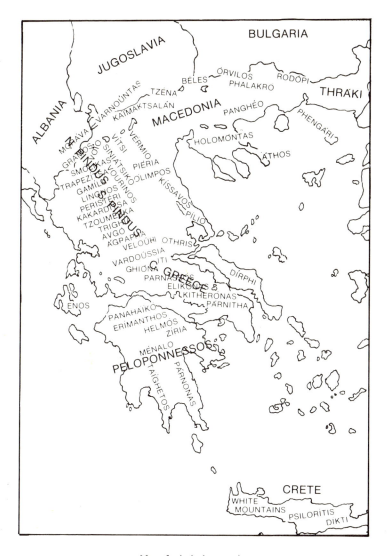

Map of principal mountains

The Agraphiotis river in Southern Pindus, a typical Greek mountain stream.

various forms. Other rock types widely present are flysch and schists, as well as serpentine and various types of volcanic rock.

Many of the Greek mountains contain sizeable deposits of a number of metals, such as bauxite, chrome, nickel, manganese and even gold. Some of these were found a long time ago and have been mined ever since; others are of more recent discovery; and yet new deposits are still being brought to light.

Caves

The Greek mountains are richly supplied with caves both large and small, which are a veritable magnet for speliologists. Many of them have

Above: Mountain trout *(Salmo trutta),* the most common fish in the Greek mountain streams. *Below:* The man-made lake of Mégdovas river in the Agrapha region.

been thoroughly explored by members of the Greek Speleological Association and individual cave lovers; others remain as yet to be investigated.

Mountain streams and lakes

In some of the Greek mountains, especially in Crete and the Peloponnese, springs are rare, while in others there is abundant water which forms impetuous little streams which join up with others to create quite large rivers. The mountain streams are cold and fast-running-a favourite environment of the delicious mountain trout (*Salmo trutta),* as well as other fish, crayfish and river crabs.

Greece has only a few natural mountain lakes, but with the construction of various dams in recent years, several large artificial lakes have been created which give something of a Swiss look to their surroundings. These lake reservoirs are plentifully stocked with fish similar to that of the highland rivers, and are also the habitat of various types of water fowl.

MAN-MADE FACILITIES

Roads

In recent years, hundreds of kilometers of highland road have been cut through the forests covering the Greek mountains. This has resulted in unprecedented environmental changes. Aside from the damage incidental to construction as such, these roads have led to a sharp increase in poaching, illegal woodfelling, and disastrous forest fires. On the positive side, they have provided access to many previously totally isolated areas, aided communication between the mountain villages, and facilitated the rational exploitation of the forests.

Shelters

In certain highland areas where rare animals gather, or which are special beauty spots, the State has constructed mountain shelters. They are not guarded however, and this, together with the uncivilised

The ski centre on Mt Velouhi (Tymphristós) in Central Greece.

behaviour of many trippers and the spread of poaching, has unfortunately resulted in the shelters not functioning as they were intended—i.e. as a means of protection for the local animals and their natural environment.

Highland tourism and ski centers

There have been intense efforts in recent years to develop winter sports and highland tourism in Greece. This has meant the building of winter sports centres on many of the Greek mountains, with the construction of a good many more still to come. Some of these centres are to be warmly recommended, others are still operating at a very primitive level.

Hostels

In the area from Macedonia to Crete there are roughly 50 mountain hostels. Of these, about 40 are the property of the National Ski and Alpine Federation, which has local branches throughout Greece; the remainder are run by various excursion and mountaineering clubs. Most of the hostels have no guards living on the premises, and are in use only when visited by mountaineers. Since the construction of so many new roads in the mountains they have lost much of their original character and receive many casual day trippers, especially in the summer months.

THE ENVIRONMENT

The climate

The Greek mountains as a whole vary greatly in their climatic conditions, depending on altitude and geographical latitude. Generally speaking, they extend over three climatic zones which directly are related to their elevation: the semi-highland, the highland, and the alpine belt.

The semi-highland belt begins where the plains end: it stretches from the foothills to a height of approximately 800 m, though on certain northern slopes this might be no more than 500 m. The climate here is characterised by long hot and dry long, summers, and short mild winters. Spring and autumn arrive somewhat suddenly and are of short duration.

The highland belt lies above the semi-highland belt, extending up to about 2,000 m. Here the summers are relatively short and the winters longer. Snowfalls are frequent from December to April, and very frequently during January and February. Spring and autumn are usually accompanied by considerable rain, which alternates with bright sunny days.

The alpine zone lies above 2,000 m, and its climate resembles that of the most northerly tundra. The summers generally last no more than two months, and even then the temperature rarely rises above 25° Centigrade and falls very considerably at night. In these regions, spring and autumn are of brief duration, but winter is long and accompanied by a great deal

The mountain hostel in the Varvára locality on Mt Taýgetos.

of snow. For at least three months of the year, from January to March, the ground in the alpine zone is solidly covered with a thick layer of snow or pack-ice, but the first snowfalls begin as early as November, and the last patches of snow do not melt until June.

The flora

Any even half-observant person climbing up a mountain will notice that the vegetation changes with altitude. The species of plant which were abundant at the beginning of the trek slowly fade out and disappear

17

altogether the higher the elevation, giving way to other species which did not exist lower down. This effect is basically due to the climatic differences between one zone and the next.

The semi-highland zone, with its long dry summers and mild winters, has the type of vegetation known as *maquis* generally tough scrubland plants able to survive the long waterless summers. In the *maquis* we find various species of evergreen shrub, such as the strawberry tree *(Arbutus unedo)*, holm oak *(Quercus ilex)*, kerm oak *(Quercus coccifera)*, mock privet *(Phyllirea media)*, alder buckthorn *(Rhamnus frangula)*. and others. Alongside these grow woody plants like thyme, cistus, butcher's broom *(Ruscus)* etc. All of the above have very long roots which penetrate deeply among the stones and rocks in search of even the slightest trace of moisture. The trees in this zone are pines such as the Aleppo pine *(Pinus halepensis)*, Italien cypress *(Cupressus sempervirens)*, and Phoenician juniper *(Juniperus phoenicea)*.

Other plants of the semi-highland zone are those with bulbs or tubers -e.g. wild cyclamen *(Cyclamen graecum)*, sternbergia *(Sternbergia sicula)*, gladiolus *(Gladiolus segetum)*, anemones *(Anemone pavonina)* etc. These usually flower in either spring or autumn, their foliage above ground drying up in the summer. The same is true of the self-seeding annuals such as poppies *(Papaver rhoeas)*, wild marguerites *(Anthemis)*, chamomile *(Matricaria chamonila)* and others.

Higher up in the highland zone, the vegetation still keeps changing and the prickly and evergreen shrubs give place to various kinds of deciduous trees to begin with, and higher up still to such species as black pine *(Pinus nigra)* and Greek fir *(Abies cephallonica)*. Many of the mountains, especially in Northern Greece, are covered with forests of deciduous trees instead of pines, with beeches, sweet chestnuts, maples and similar species.

In the highland zone, where big forest trees afford them some shelter, or in the clearings protected by trees all round and in the meadows, beautiful shrubs are to be found, such as the different kinds of wild rose, of honeysuckle and hawthorn. This is also the habitat of some of the most astonishingly lovely wild flowers of Greece: lilies *(Lilium martagon and L. chalcedonicum)*, and the truly exquisite peonies *(Paeonia mascula, P. peregrina* etc.).

Spring comes late to the highland zone. The first flowers, such as the crocus *(Crocus sieberi, C. olivierii*, etc.), are out from March onwards, but most of the other wild flowers prefer to wait until April or May. Even June is still considered a spring month at this altitude.

A spring visit to the forests of this zone remains unforgettable. The gorges and valleys are a sea of tender green with poplars, planes, willows and Norway maples all decked out in their fresh new leaves. Mountain streams roar and tumble frothily down from the snow-covered peaks; on their banks grow cranesbill, campanula, columbine and violets. Here and

Wild flowers characteristic of the Greek mountains: 1. *Lilium chalcedonium*—2. *Aubretia deltoidea*—3. *Anemone blanda*—4. *Sencecio macedonicus*—5. *Malcolmia serbica*—6. *Iris pumila s. sp. attica.*

there among the trees are clusters of pale yellow primroses or a striking orchrys, a delicate blue wood anemone, or big clusters of virginia stock growing from fissures in the rock.

Further up still, where the forest ends and even the bare grassland has petered out among the first rocks of the distant peaks, is the beginning of the alpine zone with its long harsh winters and almost non-existent summers. As the snow begins to melt from May onwards, many flowers make their first appearance, though the majority prefer to flower rather later when the weather is much better.

The variety of wild flowers in the alpine zone is very considerable. Of the roughly 600 endemic species of the Greek flora, about 400 are plants of this zone. Here plants will grow which are also to be found in the Alps and in the mountains of the Balkans and Asia Minor. Some, like crocus and gentian, prefer open meadows, others favour more rocky locations, for instance saxifrage and houseleek, others yet grow in the vicinity of springs and streams, such as kingcup and crow's foot. But all of these plants require a cold climate and cannot survive in the temperatures at lower altitudes.

Just as the plant species of the *maquis* have developed mechanisms to help them withstand the heat—densely hairy of shiny leathery surfaces to limit moisture loss—so the plants of the alpine zone, which are in general smaller, have their own protective characteristics to ensure that they will get through the cold. The majority of them die back during the winter, keeping only their bulbs or tubers alive which are protectively hidden in some rock fissure or under a stone. Others have evolved a hard dense foliage which forms a compact, cushion which wards off the winter cold from the roots. The annuals, which die altogether, ensure survival by freely scattering their tough little seeds in the autumn, which then lie dormant on the ground until moisture and spring sun make them germinate and grow into a new generation of the plant in the following year.

The fauna

The Greek mountains provide the habitat for a host of animals, insects, reptiles and birds, the species of which are interdependent and form complex ecological communities, or ecosystems.

Unfortunately, the increased hunting and ever more accurate shooting,of recent years, as well as the destruction of large tracts of forest by fires, has brought many of the species of the local fauna to the brink of extinction. The large mammals and especially the birds of prey are in the most immediate danger.

The most ubiquitous mammal of the Greek mountains is the hare, which can be found almost everywhere from the scrublands of the semi-highland zone to the alpine meadows, from Crete to Thrace. The red

1. Among the most beautiful, but also the most endangered of the Greek mountain flowers are the peonies. Illustrated, *Paeonia mascula s. sp. hellenica.*—2. Another rare plant of the Greek mountains, *Viola delphinantha.*—3. *Tulipa montana,* one of the many wild species of tulip to be found in the Greek mountains.

The chamois *(Rupicapra rupicapra)* is one of the most attractive, but also the rarest of the mammals in the Greek mountains. It inhabits rocky locations, the precipitous nature of which keeps its enemies at bay.

fox is another common species, usually frequenting the lower altitudes where the shrubs and bushes afford it concealment when hunting for its food.

The wolf, which once existed plentifully even in the Peloponnese, has become restricted to Northern and Central Greece. It prefers to live in isolated forests in the highland zone, but in winter, where there is a scarcity of food, it comes boldly down to the villages to attack the sheep.

Still quite common is the wild boar which roams many of the mountains in Northern and Central Greece in considerable numbers. Even intensive hunting has not much affected the distribution of wild boars because they reproduce quickly and readily adapt to any environment.

The brown bears which once lived on all of the Greek mountains are less fortunate. Those that still exist have withdrawn into the depths of only the most inapproachable forests in the Pindus range and the mountains of Greece's northern borders. They have become a protected

Author's painting of the lammergeyer (*Gypaetus barbatus*), the largest bird in the Greek mountains and in all of Europe.

species which it is strictly forbidden to hunt, and there are indications that their numbers may be slowly increasing again.

The lynxes, which were extremely common once upon a time, now live only in the stony valley of the Aóos river in the Pindus range and in the border forests.

Also in the northern mountains there are many roe-deer, inhabiting the dense forests of the highland zone. Red deer, on the other hand, have almost disappeared and can only be found now sparsely distributed in the highland-zone forests on the borders with Yugoslavia and Bulgaria, and there are a few left on Mt Párnitha in Attica.

A rare species are the chamois. They keep together in small herds in precipitous rocky locations where they can easily escape from predatory carnivores. In summer they climb up to the most exposed heights, while in winter they descend to the ravines and gullies for shelter. There are not many of them left today, thinly scattered on Mt Vardoúsia, Mt Oíti, Mt Ghióna, Mt Ólympos, Mt Gamila, Mt Smólikas, and on one or two other mountains in the north.

A relative of the chamois on the mainland is the Cretan wild goat *(Capra aegagrus cretensis),* a unique species which today is only found in the Gorge of Samariá in southern Crete and nowhere else in the world. Although it is a strictly protected species now, it is still in danger from poachers, as is also its cousin, the wild goat of Samothráce, which lives on Mt Phengári.

Jackals are to be found in the *maquis* scrublands of the semi-highland zone, where they feed on carrion and small animals. They are completely harmless.

Special mention should also be made of the wild cat, which is in great danger of total extinction. There are only very few of these animals left today, with the dense forests of Northern Greece as their last refuge.

Other, smaller animals who make their homes in the Greek mountains are the beech marten, the European badger, the red squirrel, the shrew, spalax and mole among others.

Of the 56 kinds of Greek birds of prey, 50 or so live either entirely or predominantly in the mountains. Amongst them are the different species of eagle, two species of vulture, and a host of other, smaller birds. The biggest bird of prey to be found in the Greek mountains and indeed in all of Europe, is the lammergeyer *(Gypaetus barbatus)*, which subsists mainly on the carcasses of smaller animals.

The forests of the highland zone are the habitat of a myriad of large and small insect and seed-eating birds: the stockdove, cuckoo, blackbird, thrush, chaffinch, various dippers and tits, the crossbill, crow, magpie and others. In the lower-lying scrublands there are robins, crested larks, goldfinches, etc. The alpine zone has certain birds which rarely descend to the lower altitudes. Among then are the snowfinch *(Montifringilla nivalis),* the alpine chough *(Pyrrhocorax graculus)* and the chough *(Fringilla montifringilla),* shore lark *(Eremorphilia alpestris),* and alpine swift *(Apus melba).*

Griffon vultures *(Gyps fulvus)* are still quite common in the mountains of Northern Greece.

The Greek mountains also harbour a considerable variety of reptiles (snakes and lizards) on which little research has been done so far. The only endangered species at the moment seems to be the viper in its various sub-species.

The insects too have so far been neglected by the scientists, although there is every indication that the Greek mountains are one of the richest areas in this respect in all of Europe.

The Spanish lynx (Lynx pardinus), which used to be common in all of mainland Greece and is now in danger of extinction. The few remaining animals live in shy concealment in the Pindus and Rhodopi ranges.

ETHNOGRAPHY

The Peoples

The mountain slopes of the Greek highlands are dotted with many villages to about 1,500 m altitude, and solitary shepherds make their living in the alpine zone all through the summer months. They take their flocks of sheep up in spring, and remain in the mountain pastures until the winter forces them down into the villages again.

In ethnographic terms, the population of the mountains of Southern Greece is considered pure Greek, whereas in the north some of the people and whole communities, though fully hellenised today, are of non-Greek origins.

The Vlachs: These were once a Latin-speaking people whose language very much resembles both Romanian and Italian. Perhaps they were stragglers from the Roman legions. Another of the several conflicting surmises as to their origins and reason for settling in Greece is that they were an indigenous people who had already been living for a long time in

1. The Vlachs of Métsovo still retain their old language, costumes and customs.—2. The majority of the inhabitants of the Pindus range are fair-haired.—3. A Greek at the time of the revolution against the Turks.—4. Christian Albanian from Souli, at the time of the revolution.

the heart of the Balkan peninsula when they became latinised during the era of the Roman occupation of what is today's Romania. Yet another theory considers them a nomadic tribe from Vlahia, Romania, who spread into Bulgaria, Macedonia, the Pindus etc. in search of grazing lands for their cattle.

There are Vlachs in many of the villages in the Pindus range, in Eastern Zagóri for instance and around Métsovo, where the Vlach language is now spoken by only a few of the oldest inhabitants.

The Albanians: This is a very old race which at one time extended all over the western Balkans. During the period of the Ottoman Empire, the Albanians spread southwards from what is today Albania through Greece to the slopes of Mt Taýgetus and Mt Parnassós, forced to leave their homes because the Turks had split their country into Muslim and Christian areas. To avoid persecution from Albanian and Turkish Muslims alike, the Christian Albanians mass-emigrated south and settled in Attica, Argolis, the Saronic islands, the Peloponnese and elsewhere in Greece.

The most renowned of the Albanians were the Souliótes, who lived in the mountains of Souli in Épirus and distinguished themselves by their struggles against the powerful and notorious Ali Pasha of Ioánnina. When the War of Independence against the Turks broke out in 1821, the Christian Albanians sided with the Greeks, and have ever since identified their fortunes with those of Greece and have become Greek citizens.

The Saracatsánoi: These used to be a nomadic people who eventually settled in scattered communities on the northern mountains from Thrace to Thessaly. They are said to be one of the purest Greek tribes, and are universally acknowledged to be of very ancient origin. According to one theory, they were a pre-Hellenic Pelasgian tribe who for some reason or other had to withdraw deep inland into the mountains.

The Karagoúnoi: This is probably a branch of the Vlachs, now living in scattered small pockets in the mountains of Épirus, Thessaly and Central Greece. They are also known as "Arvanitóvlachoi"—Albanian Vlachs—because they often lived side by side with the Albanians. Their own name for their tribe was "Romans". Such remnants as still exist of them today have been totally absorbed into the Greek population.

Traditional settlements

During the years of the Ottoman Empire, the geographic location of many highland communities contributed to their being left alone by the Turks, who had little love for the wild mountain areas where anything could happen. As a result of this neglect, the Greek communities flourished economically and culturally, and there was considerable commerce with places as far away as Romania, Italy, Odessa and Constantinople. Some of the Greeks specialised as transporters, with caravans of mules numbering hundreds of animals; in other villages the accent was on various forms of traditional arts and crafts. The overall prosperity led to

Above: Houses in Makrinítsa, one of the most beautiful villages in the Mt Pílion area.
Below: Interior of the Tossitsas mansion in Métsovo.

the development of architecture, and fine two and three-storey mansions began to appear among the poorer village houses. At the same time, donations from the wealthier inhabitants made it possible to build for the public benefit, and bridges, churches, schools, viaducts and roads were constructed. These projects were all executed by teams of skilled country artisans who travelled from village to village as required.

The great majority of these testimonies to the civilisation of the Greek country people no longer exist. In the last war, around a thousand Greek villages were destroyed by the Italian and German conquerors. Even after the war had ended the destruction continued, either by the population deserting their villages for the towns or for abroad in search for work, or by the progress of modernisation.

The main areas where traditional highland settlements can still be seen today are on Mt Pílion and in Western Zagóri in Epirus. The Pílion villages are justly famous for their splendid mansions in the Thessalian-Macedonian style, like basilicas having three main rooms side by side one another, and with their walls and ceilings decorated by folk painters of the time.

The village of Makrinítsa is of particularly great architectural interest, and accordingly has been placed under State protection for the maintenance of its architectural treasures. In the region of Western Zagóri, all the buildings are made of the local grey stone. The most interesting villages in this part of the Pindus are Vítsa, Koukoúli, Negádes, Pápingo and Monodéndri. The last two have also been placed under State protection as of particular historical value to the nation. Especially noteworthy are the churches of the Zagóri villages, built in the style of basilicas, usually with interior arcades on both sides of the central area, and extremely beautifully carved wooden altar screens.

HISTORY

The Greek mountains have played a significant role in the country's history, particularly so in more recent times. When the Turks began to overrun the Greek peninsula in the fifteenth century, many highland communities managed to negotiate certain privileges, mainly economic, in return for judicious surrender. In time, this resulted in commercially and culturally flourishing communities on the flanks of many Greek mountains—in sharp contrast to the primitive life in the villages on the plains which were more directly under the rule of the Turks, who in no way concerned themselves with the educational or cultural needs of their subjects.

The villages of the Pílion peninsula, those on Mt Gamíla in the Pindus range, in the vine-growing areas on the slopes of Mts Kíssavos and Siátista in Western Macedonia, the Vlach communities of Syráko and Kalarítes on Mt Kakardítsa in the Southern Pindus, and other highland

Above: Old bridge at Zagóri (Epirus). *Below:* Loom in the village of Neráida in the Southern Pindus.

communities in different areas of the country thus grew into centres of learning with schools and libraries and kept the Greek heritage alive.

While the villages in the northern mountains became custodians of civilisation, those in the south—the Máni on the southern flanks of Mt Taýetos and the Sfakiá region in the White Mountains in Crete—rather became strongholds of freedom. These villages retained a fierce and unquenchable spirit of independence, exploiting to the full the privileges granted them by the Turks from the beginning, which their geographical location made it inadvisable for the pashas to challenge.

The increasing decline of the Ottoman Empire from the sixteenth century onwards went hand in hand with an ever harsher administration of the Balkan subject peoples by the Porte. The level of taxes went up continually, and non-payment resulted in brutal counter-measures. It was at this time that the first rebels, the famous klepht ("thieves") made their appearance in the Greek mountain communities.

> *I can't, mother, I can't*
> *work for the Turks.*
> *I'll take my gun*
> *and join the klepht*

Many of the young men of the mountain villages bid goodbye forever to their homes and their families to enter on the hard life of the outlaw. They lived in bands deep in the forests and in caves high up in the mountains Harsh as their life was, and all its dangers notwithstanding, it was at least free. In the depths of their hearts the klephts must have felt a certain contempt for the timid people of the towns and on the plains, and would not have changed their rough existence for any urban comforts under the nose of the hated Turks.

Another type of Greek rebel were the armatoloí armed mountain bands. Their leaders were Greeks whom the Turks, who had little love for these wild areas, had prudently appointed to administer local Greek affairs. The areas where they operated were known as the armatolíka, where they were obliged to levy the taxes for the Turkish overlords, and where they formed armed bands to protect themselves against the klephts. The office of armatolós was frequently passed on from father to son, so that in time the armatoloí became a kind of warning aristocracy.

Frequently there were armed clashes between the klepht and the armatoloí. However, it was not unusual for a captain of the klepht who was willing to surrender to be rewarded by the Turks with a position as armatolós, while a defeated armatolós often took to the mountains to become a klepht. For this reason the difference between klepht and armatoloí was rather blurred in the popular imagination, as demonstrated in the following song, which also expresses the love of these mountain

Typical mansion in the village of Monodéndri near the Víkos gorge.

people for their natural surroundings, of which they felt themselves to be an integral part.

> *I would like to be a shepherd in May, a vintner in August,*
> *and in the heart of winter a tavernkeeper selling wine.*
> *But better still to be an armatolós and a klepht,*
> *an armatolós in the mountains and a klepht in the plains,*
> *to have the rocks as my brothers, the trees as my relatives,*
> *put to sleep by partridges, woken by nightingales,*
> *and the summit of Liákoura as my place of worship.*

(Liákoura is another name for Mt Parnassós, the highest peak of which is still known by that name today.)

When the revolution finally broke out in earnest in 1821, the armatoloí joined up with the klepht who came down from the mountains and they fought side by side in their common aspiration for freedom. After countless sacrifices, they and other revolutionaries liberated a small part of the ‘Greek peninsula from the Turks, and this small heartland was the beginning of the modern Greek State.

The next mountain epic in Greek history was the 1940-41 Greek-Italian war. Mussolini launched an unprovoked attack on Greece across the borders of Albania, which at this time had been virtually incorporated into Italy. The Italians surged over the Pindus range, expecting to descend quickly into Greece, at least as far as Ioánnina. However, they had reckoned without the fierce determination of the Greek army and the whole of the Greek people to defend their country, and the jaunty Italian advance rapidly turned in a rout as the front was pushed back from the Greek to the Albanian mountains.

This presented the first victory against the seemingly invincible Axis force in World War II, and Greece is justly proud of it. Unfortunately, no proper advantage was taken of the utter defeat of the Italians. Although the Greek army could at this point have driven them into the sea, the General Staff kept it immobilised in the Pindus mountains of Albania. During that winter many of the Greek soldiers were maimed by frostbite or killed outright by the bitter cold and from lack of supplies, but they never lost their high morale and went on hoping for better things to come.

Furious with *il Duce* for having tainted the image of Axis invincibility, Hitler sent German troops to the rescue. They came across Yugoslavia, (stimulating the heroic resistance of the Yugoslavs and swept into Greece, to Salonica and down to Athens, the body of the Greek army meanwhile, remaining undefeated in the Albanian and Pindus mountains.

At this crucial hour the General Staff could think of nothing better than to capitulate, and the Greek soldiers, without another shot being fired, had to surrender to the same enemy forces they had decisively beaten only a few weeks earlier. In appreciation of the fighting spirit of the Greek soldiers, the Germans did not take them prisoner, and left them to get back to their homes as well they could. Many of these men kept and hid their weapons after they had finally arrived back at their villages, having

One of the most renowned warrior captains of the 1821 Revolution, Odysseus Androutsos, who was also known as "the Lion of Roumeli" (Central Greece).

been helped on the way with food and shelter by Greek villagers. These weapons came in useful again later when the Greek resistance movement became organised.

The Germans shared the occupation of Greece with their Italian and Bulgarian allies, and began their regime of mass transportations, imprisonment and executions. In 1941 the Greek people were dying of hunger, and especially in the towns and cities it was no unusual sight to see men and women and children fall down dead in the street, victims of starvation. Meanwhile in the Greek mountains the resistance movement grew apace. The Roúmeli mountains of Central Greece were riddled with

35

Greek resistance fighters in the mountains of Central Greece at the time of the German occupation of the country during World War II.

hide-outs of resistance groups. Similar bands appeared later in the Pindus range, the mountains of the Peloponnese, of Crete, and Macedonia.

From 1942 onwards, the Greek guerrillas made themselves more and more felt, and had the support of the great majority of the Greek people. Acts of sabotage and attacks against the occupying forces became an almost everyday occurrence. In the mountain hide-outs, spirits were high:

> *There is thunder on Ólympus and lightning on Ghióna,*
> *Ágrapha and Stereá are groaning for revenge.*
> *To arms, to arms, take up the fight*
> *for what is dearest of all*—for liberty!

It was not long before the Italian army surrendered to their former allies, the Germans. However, many of the Italians preferred to fall into the hands of the Greek guerrillas, rather than be taken by the Germans. They brought with them large quantities of arms and ammunition, and in this way the Greek resistance fighters acquired even artillery.

In time, the Greek resistance groups in the mountains became one of the strongest of the guerrilla forces in Europe, and played an effective

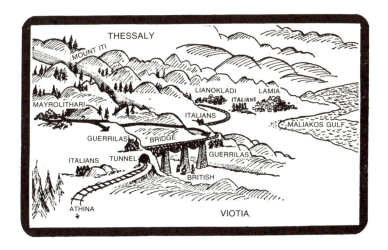

The destruction of the Gorgopotamos river bridge one night by Greek resistance fighters and English intelligence units was one of the major acts of sabotage of World War II.

part in wearing down the Axis powers. In 1944 the Germans had to abandon Greece, with Greek fighters following close on their heels and harrowing their retreat.

Close behind the retreating Germans arrived the British. The civil war which broke out shortly afterwards ended with the defeat of the left-wing guerrillas on the peaks of Mt Grámmos in the Northern Pindos range.

MYTHOLOGY

The mountains of Greece feature prominently in Greek mythology. Impressed by the supreme grandeur of Mt Ólympos, the ancient Greeks made it the residence of their great pantheon of twelve, presided over by Zeus and Hera.

Mt Díkti in Crete was said to have sheltered Rhea, who was hiding the infant Zeus from his father Cronos, who had the objectionable habit of

37

swallowing his children to prevent them from usurping his power one day. Young Zeus was raised on the milk of the goat Amalthéa and when he grew up, got rid of his unnatural father and ruled the world.

Mt Ida in Southern Phrygia was the mountain where Paris, son of Priam and Hecuba, was exposed as an infant because of a prophecy that he would bring ruin on the House of Troy. Fate not being so easily thwarted, he was found, however, and brought up by shepherds. He fell in love with the nymph Oenóna, but deserted her to eventually elope the lovely Helen from the Greeks. From the summit of Mt Ida, Zeus later watched the battles of the Trojan War, fought to recapture the much-courted Helen, herself a daughter of Zeus by Leda.

Mt Parnassós in Central Greece is famous as the mountain of Apollo, god of light. On the slopes of this mountain—the navel of the earth, according to the ancient Greeks—stood the great temple to this god, which was also the seat of the famous Delphic oracle of Apollo.

It was also on Mt Parnassós that Deucalion, son of Prometheus, came to rest with his ark when the great flood subsided by which Zeus had destroyed the sons of man for their sins. There Deucalion and his wife Pyrrha sacrificed to Zeus. On oracular advice they threw stones over their shoulders, and from those thrown by Deucalion sprang up men, and those thrown by Pyrrha turned into women. In this way the human race was replenished. It was presumably by more orthodox means that Deucalion and Pyrrha later became the parents of Hellen, the legendary ancestor of the entire Hellenic race and the father of all the Greek tribes.

It was believed to have been on the summit of MtTaýgetos where Zeus, in the shape of a swan, coupled with Leda who subsequently gave birth to the Dioscuri, Castor and Pollux, brothers of Helen of Troy. This mountain was also the favourite of Artemis, goddess of the hunt, who liked to wander in the forests there, as well as in those on Mt Erýmanthos in the Northern Peloponnese.

Mt Pangaío in Eastern Macedonia is renowned for having been the mountain climbed by the lyre-playing Orpheus to worship Apollo in his aspect as god of music. When the Thracian Maenads, votaries of Dionysus, who roamed the mountain in their ecstasies, inadvertently came across Orpheus, they tore him to pieces in one of their intoxicated frenzies.

Mt Oíti in Central Greece (frequently rendered in English as Oeta) was the place where the legendary Hercules finally met his end—on the peak appropriately enough called Pyrá. Married to Deiánira, Hercules was nevertheless moved to carry off the beautiful Ióle of Oecholia. His wife sent him a tunic smeared with the blood of the centaur Nessus whom Hercules had killed years earlier, which was supposed to magically win back her husband's love. But the blood had been poisoned by the Hydra which Hercules had despatched shortly before killing Nessus, and as soon as he put on the tunic it caused him fearful suffering. Since he could not tear it off his flesh, he had himself carried up Mt Oíti and placed on a pyre. After bequeathing the lovely Ióle to his son, he had the pyre set alight, and was

The death of Orpheus.

carried to heaven and rewarded for his previous exploits by marriage to
the goddess Hebe, daughter of Hera.

Mt Pílion is another mountain frequently mentioned in the ancient
myths. It was there that Cyréne lived, a nymph devoted to the hunt, as well
as the wise centaur Chiron. One day Apollo was idly watching Cyréne
struggling with a líon and fell violently in love with her. On the advice of
Chiron he married her, and from their union Aristáeus was born, who was
a god of various kinds of husbandry and, in his mother's honour, of
hunting. It was he, also, who persuaded the gods to let the meltemi blow
in the Cyclades islands, an annual wind which blows for forty days in July
and August, relieving the heat and driving the mills to grind the corn.

Chiron's cave was an academy of learning for many of the heroes of the
Argonaut expedition to recover the Golden Fleece, foremost among them

Jason. Here also lived the hero Pilioas, brother of Aïantha of Salamina, who eventually gave his name to the mountain.

Mt Pílion was also the site of the great battle of the centaurs with the lapithae, which was provoked by the improper behaviour of the centaurs at the wedding feast of the lapith king Pirithos with Hippodamia.

Other inhabitants of the mountains were dryads, naiads and oreads, nymphs of the trees, rivers and mountains respectively. They were not immortal, but very long-lived. The dryads were said to live for as long as the tree that had happened to germinate at the moment they were born. Close by—rather too close by for the nymphs' comfort at times— gambolled the rudely rumbustious satyrs, fertility spirits of the woods and hills, and the rather gentler fauns who had human shape except for horses' legs and tails and pointed ears. Fauns were the only creatures who could become the nymphs' lovers.

The god *par excellence* of the woods and the mountains was Pan, whose lower limbs were those of a goat. He was originally a local deity of Mt Ménnalon in Arcadia. It was he who invented the musical pipe of seven reeds which he called Syrinx after an unattainable nymph he loved. He was a relatively gentle creature, nevertheless the nameless apprehension which can overcome travellers in lonely mountain places was named after him—panic fear. He also hopelessly loved the nymphs Pitys and Echo, who fled from him and were changed, the one into a pine tree, the other into a voice which repeats only the last word.

Not only in antiquity, but even in more recent times the Greek people have created myths about their mountains. One of these explains how the mighty Pindus range acquired its name.

Once upon a time there was a prince, Pindus by name, who left his father's court to live in the forests to hunt. Here he met dragon, and every time he bagged some game, they shared it between them. The monster and the Prince became great friends. When Pindus' father died, his wicked younger brother made himself king. Afraid that Pindus would return some day to claim his rightful throne, the new king sought him out in the forest and killed him. When the dragon happened to pass and saw his friend lying dead, he rushed with a dragon fury at the wicked brother and his company and tore them all into ribbons. Ever since then the mountains where all this took place have been known as the Pindus mountains.

Another post-classical myth is told about two small lakes high up in the mountains, the one on Mt Gamíla and the other on Mt Smólika, also in the Pindus. These lakes are called dragon lakes because in the deep black waters of each there used to live a solitary dragon. They were very quarrelsome neighbours, and the tale concerns itself with the tree trunks one of them hurled at his rival from forest-covered Mt Smólikas and the rocks with which the other retaliated from bare and stony Mt Gamíla.

THE GREEK MOUNTAINS IN FOLK POETRY

All through the ages the Greek people have continued to be deeply attached to their mountains, and out of their awe, admiration and love grew endless folk stories, folk songs and poems, composed and remembered by the Greek mountain people. They portray the mountains as living entities, able to feel happiness, anger, or sorrow, and simultaneously pay tribute to the birds and flowers, the forests and highland glens, the rivers and the snow-covered peaks.

The song below refers to the father of Odysseus Androútsos, a hero of the revolution, who left the mountains of Roúmeli and went as far away as the Southern Peloponnese to fight in the unsuccessful early revolution of 1770.

The black mountains are weeping, they are without consolation,
they weep not for their height, they weep not for their sorrows,
but because the klepht have abandoned them for the plains.

Mt Ghióna says to Mt Liákoura and Mt Liákoura to Mt Ghióna:
"Brother mountain, you are higher and see further,
where are they, what has happened to the klephts?
Where are they slaughtering their lambs for the feast?
Which mountains are they decorating now with Turkish head ?"

"What can I tell you, brother mountain, what can I tell you, friend.
The mangy plains are enjoying our brave young heroes,
it's in the plains where they're slaughtering their lambs for the feast,
it is the plains that are resplendent now with Turkish heads."

Hearing this, Mt Liákoura feels heavy and anguished with sorrow.
He looks to the left, to the right, down into the plain and calls:
"You sickly plain down there, you withered plain,
you think you'll wear the glory of my heroes?
Caste off your finery, give me back my braves,
or I'll melt all my snows and turn you into a lake!"

The next poem speaks of the big Kolokotrónis family whose armed bands constituted the largest of the rebel forces in the Peloponnesian mountains at the time of the Turks.

The sunset, the evening star and the moon laughed at me
as I went by night up the mountains, high up on the peaks.
I heard the wind quarrelling with the moutains.
"You mountains, high mountains, and you foothills,
why are you quarrelling, what is making you so angry?
Are the waters and the load of the snow troubling you?"
"It isn't the waters or the load of the snow that trouble us,
the only thing troubling us are the klepht , the Kolokotrónoi."

41

Here is a song about Yánní Boukouválas, appointed captain of warriors of Roumeli and Epirus, who in the middle of the eighteenth century fought with the Mousouhousái Albanians from whom Ali Pasha of Ioánnina was descended. The Albanian Muslims are often referred to in the songs as Turks.

What is the shouting and the uproar about
In the open spaces of the village of Kerásovo?
Boukouválas is fighting with the Mousouhousái
The bullets are falling like hail and the mountains cry out in pain.

A little bird calls from a high branch:
"Stop the war, Yánni, stop your shooting
for the dust to settle and the andartes to rise,
to count the klephts, to count the Turks!"
When the Turks have three times been counted, they are five hundred
fewer,
When the klephts have been counted, they are three heroes less.

Nikotsáras was one of the armed mountain chiefs, an armatolós of Elassóna at the end of the eighteenth century. When Ali Pasha deprived him of his office, he became a klepht and wrought havoc and much destruction among the Turks. He even organised a small fleet of kaïques with which he raided the Macedonian coast. In 1806, when the Russo-Turkish war broke out, Nikotsáras arranged with the Russian admiral Siniavin that he would cross Macedonia and Bulgaria, and hit the Turkish army in Romania from the south. The plan failed, but Nikotsáras managed to fight his way back to the coast and finally reached safety in Àghio Óros.

What's the matter with the Zíchna mountains, why are they drooping?
Is the hail hitting them, is the winter too heavy?
Neither is hail hitting them, nor is winter too heavy,
Nikotsáras is fighting against three districts,
Zíchna, Hántakas, and the wastes of Právi.
Three days he's been fighting, three days and three nights,
Without bread, without water, without closing his eyes.
They ate snow, they drank snow, and kept up the flame.

The next song refers to the arrest of the revolutionary hero Katsantónis, who subsequently died a martyr's death in Ioánnina.

Good health to you, high mountains and cool springs,
to you, Tzoumérka and Àgrapha, refuge for warriors.
If you see my wife, if you see my son,
tell them I was caught by treachery and ill luck.
They found me sick and unarmed on my pallet,
like a helpless babe in his rocking cradle.

Here Mt Ólympos confronts the much lower Mt Kíssavos, the peaks of which are easily accessible to the Turks:

Mt Ólympos and Mt Kíssavos are quarrelling
over which will make rain and which will make snow.
And Kissavos lets it rain, and Ólympos lets it snow.
Then Ólympos turns round and says to Kíssavos:
"Don't make me angry, Kíssavos, you who are walked on by Turks,
trodden by Turks and Aghas from Lárissa.
I am great Ólympos, famous throughout the world.
I have forty-two peaks and sixty-two springs,
and each of my peaks flies a flag, every tree hides a klepht."

Euboea has pleasant low mountains, including Mt Xerovoúni, the highest point, in the photograph (1,417 m).

43

Mt Dourdouvána in the Peloponnese can be considered an offshoot of Mt Hélmos. Its flanks are covered with large woods of Cephallonian fir and black pines.

Part II
THE MOUNTAINS

NOTE The approximate walking times given are only valid in the summer months when there is no snow to contend with.

To climb the border mountains, permission should be obtained from either the police or local army headquarters.

The official Greek mountaineering magazine *Vounó* has unfortunately ceased publication. As a substitute, the Greek Alpine Club of Athens (corner of Ermou St with Kapnikareas Sq) brings out an information bulletin *«Enimerotikó Deltio»* to which foreign mountaineers can send accounts of their climbs on the Greek mountains for publication.

THE PINDUS RANGE

The Pindus range is the largest of the Greek mountain formations, and indeed one of the largest in all of the Balkans. It stretches from Mt Moráva, on Albanian soil, across Greece as far as the Ágrapha range in Central Greece.

The Pindus has some of the country's highest and most beautiful mountains, as well as a great many lower peaks. The Métsovo pass divides the range into the Northern and the Southern Pindus. The latter includes the Ágrapha mountains which, with their dozens of peaks, form a mountain range of their own.

Starting points for expeditions into the Pindus mountains are the towns of Kónitsa, Ioánnina, Árta, Grevená and Thessalian Tríkala, as well as the village of Métsovo.

NORTHERN PINDUS RANGE

Mt Grámmos (2,520 m)

Mt Grámmos is one of the highest of the Greek mountains. Its summit is unnamed and is known simply as 2520 after its height. Its cone is the boundary between Greece and Albania, and also between the prefectures of Épirus and Macedonia.

The best time of the year for climbing Mt Grámmos is June when there are still snow patches here and there and the slopes are strewn all over with rare wild flowers. The lower parts of the mountain are covered with beautiful dense forest; its higher reaches are bare of trees but rich in pastureland and springs.

The quickest route to the top is through the village of Plykáti. This is reached by driving along the Ioánnina/Kónitsa-Eptahóri road, taking a

Mt Grámmos. *Above:* Going up to the 2520 peak which is seen in the distance. *Below:* The kiápha peak, seen from 2520.

left turn after Kónitsa along a dirt road which leads to the villages of Pirsóyanni, Voúrbianni and Gorgopótamos, finally to end up at Plykáti.

Plykáti is a prettily picturesque mountain village with stone houses and hospitable people. It has no guesthouse, but travellers are put up in private houses after consulting about the matter with the village mayor or

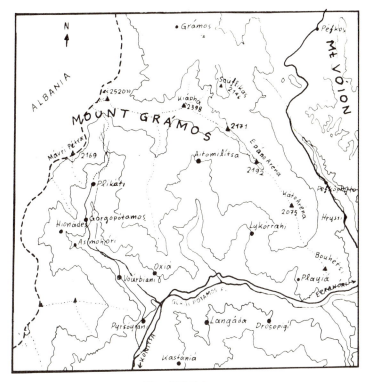

Map of Mt Grámmos.

the priest. Either of these two will also find a guide for the mountain, and a mule to carry rucksacks.

If there is no snow, the ascent from Plykáti is about four hours' straight march, not including rest periods. (Two hours should be reckoned for this.) The path first drops down to the bed of a highland stream which is fed with the frothing waters from the summit peak. Later it passes across to the opposite bank and, with the stream now on its left, steadily proceeds uphill through fallow pasture with very sparse tree cover.

Further up, the path crosses the river once more and, with the water on the right now, the steep part of the ascent begins which leads south of the 2520 peak along a ridge which joins up with the Mávri Pétra ("black rock") peak (2,168 m). This ridge forms the border between Greece and Albania. There are no guards, fences, or any visible demarkation to show where one country ends and another begins. However, the area has many demolished defence works, sad remnants of the civil war of 1949 when Mt

47

Grámmos was the last and most important stronghold of the left-wing andartes.

Going along the ridge in a northerly direction soon leads to the summit. From here the view to the west shows a gentle Albanian valley with cultivated fields. In the east lie the peaks of Grámmos Kiáfa (2,398 m) and Soúflikas (2,146 m) and lower down the unnamed 2171, and Epáno Aréna (2,192 m), and Káto Aréna (2,075 M) which juts out stark and barren from dense wild forest. In the distance in the south-west is the large Albanian Mt Nemértska, and the south is dominated by the conical mass of Mt Smólika.

The return can be either by the same route, or by a path which descends east of the summit peak and later takes a south-westerly turn towards Plykáti village.

The ascent of Mt Grámmos can also be made from the village of Aïtomylítsa on the eastern side of the mountain.

Mt Vóïo (1,802 m)

Mt Vóïo to the east of Mt Grámmos is only of medium height but very long. Its many peaks are covered in forests of beeches, black pine, firs and other trees. To make the climb to its summit, drive by the Kónitsa-Pendálophos road, and stop at a pass about 7km after the village of Eptahóri, the highest point of the road before it drops down towards Pendálophos.

From here the summit, part of a smooth, densely forested ridge, is about an hour away exactly due north of the pass. Other, lower peaks might present greater mountaineering interest, however.

Mt Smólikas (2,637 m)

Mt Smólikas is the second-highest Greek mountain, Ólympos being the first. Its summit forms a regular cone and completely dominates the surrounding area. The ascent in summer, when there is no snow, presents no particular difficulties, except for the danger of losing one's way in the dense forests which cover its flanks. The trees here are mainly black pine (*Pinus nigra*) on the lower levels, and Balkan pine (*P. heldreichii*) higher up.

The route usually taken for the ascent is from the village of Pádes, which is reached from Kónitsa. The stretch of road Kónitsa-Eléfthero-Palioséli-Pádes offers an unforgettable view of the peaks of Mt Gamíla, the bare rock faces of which plunge vertically down into the lush gully of the Aóös river.

At Pádes, accommodation is available in private houses, and the villagers will also provide a guide and pack animals. Including rest

Drakólimni lake of Mt Smólikas and the summit peak.

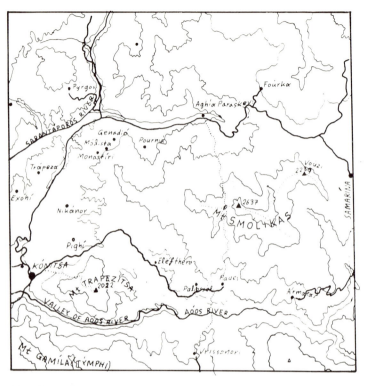

Map of part of Northern Pindus with Mts Smólikas and Trapezítsa, and the ravine of the Aóös river.

periods, the ascent takes around six-and-a-half hours which, considering the time needed for the return, requires a very early morning start.

The greater part of the trek is through forest, until a small tableland is reached. A small, very deep lake here is called Drakólimni ("dragon lake"). The location is very beautiful indeed, and can be recommended for mountain camping.

From Drakólimni, which lies at a height of 2,200 m, the ascent to the conical summit peak begins in earnest. The rock here is the reddish serpentine, which has the rare *Serpentinicola* growing on it—a great attraction for botanists. There are also pale pink heartsease *(Viola magellensis)*, bright purple campanulas, wild pinks, and many other delightful wild flowers.

The summit offers a beautiful view of the surrounding mountains—Mt Grámmos to the north, Mt Gamíla to the south—and of the seemingly

The Aóös ravine at the point where the river emerges near Kónitsa town. The summit of Mt Gamíla is seen in the distance.

endless forests which surround the peak line like an undulating sea of green.

The descent may be made by the same route, or north towards the village of Aghía Paraskeví (formerly known as Kerásovo). The route to Aghía Paraskeví goes through forests of black pine and also silver fir (*Abies pectinata*), a species common in Europe but rare in Greece.

An alternative way up the summit starts from Samarína, the highest of all Greek villages, which lies on the eastern flank of the mountain. The path from Samarína is indicated by red marks on trees, rocks etc.

Mt Trapezítsa (2,022 m)

This is a relatively small mountain, squeezed in between Mt Smólikas and Mt Gamíla, and almost completely covered with black pine and fir trees. On its slopes lies the town of Kónitsa.

The ascent begins from the upper section of Kónitsa town, following first the road towards Pádes, and turning right further along to cross some fields. The actual path begins at the foot of the mountain and leads at once into the forest. A point of identification here is a small quarry off on the right.

It is now a two-and-a-half hours' walk to the summit, where the view is magnificent. Below lies the deep gully of the river Aóös, covered in very dense, jungle-like forest. Beyond lies the peaked ridge of Mt Gamíla in all its wild grandeur, with sheer rockfaces of more than 1,000 m in height.

The descent is by the same route.

The ravine of the Aóös river

With Kónitsa as the starting point, the famous Aóös ravine can be visited, which is one of the most beautiful and completely unspoilt places in Greece. The ravine runs between Mt Gamíla and Mt Trapezítsa, and is formed by the Aóös river which springs from the Métsovo mountains.

The entrance to the ravine is very close to Kónitsa. At this point the river emerges from between the vertical rockfaces and runs down towards the plain in the direction of Albania. Exactly as its exit is the arched bridge of Kónitsa, an outstanding example of local architecture. Beside it is the modern bridge for the road from Ioánnina.

To the right of the bridge looking up the ravine is the beginning of a dirt road which runs alongside the river bed for several hundred meters. Taking this dirt road leads to a point where on the right an old path branches off which climbs up the side of the mountain. Following it for two hours through natural surroundings of magical beauty leads to the abandoned monastery Moní Stomíou.

The Aóös valley is almost virgin territory. Its very extensive forests include every species of Greek highland tree, with conifers and deciduous trees seeming to struggle for the best possible places in the crowded space. Trying to do one better than their neighbours, some even

Views in the Aóös ravine: 1. The bridge at Kónitsa.—2. Section of the ravine with the high-lying Stomíou monastery.—3. The Aóös river seen from the monastery.—4. Down in the ravine.

53

manage to find a desperate foothold among the precipitous rocks on either side.

It is here in these wild and fairy-tale forests that the last of the Greek bears live, the last of the lynxes, the wild cats, roe deer, wild boars and wolves. On the steep rock cliffs there are still chamois grazing, and vultures, eagles and lammergeyers build their nests on ledges and in crevisses of the rock. Time seems to have stood still here, and mercifully nothing has yet been heard of the area being developed for tourist interest.

It should be mentioned that the Aóös valley is part of a large National Forest which centres on the neighbouring gully of the river Víkos. Unfortunately, there is definite evidence of heavy poaching, here as well as in other National Forests, threatening various species with extinction, above all the wild bear. It is a sad but imperative duty, therefore, for any visitor who comes across a hunter to report the occurrence at once to the authorities.

The monastery Moní Stomíou has been built at the narrowest part of the valley. Looking down from a balcony, the river is seen to flow hundreds of metres below, and high, high above towers the awesome summit of Mt Gamíla, the flat bare rockface of which plunges straight down into the valley like a gigantic axe.

A small path leads to a spring a little beyond the monastery, where there is a clearing large enough for mountain camping.

The return route to Kónitsa is made along the same way.

The Víkos gorge

Greece has two great and unforgettable gorges: the gorge of Samariá in Crete, and that of the Víkos in Épirus. It is hard to decide which is the more beautiful of the two, since each is unique in its way. In my view, however, Víkos takes the prize, as much for its grandeur and wildness as for the rare treasures of its flora.

The Víkos gorge lies north-west of Mt Gamíla, and is about 10 km long. It starts half-way between the villages of Monodéndri and Koukoúli and ends to one side of Víkos village, running from south-east to north-west. Roughly in the middle it meets with another ravine, Méga Lákko, which descends from a north-easterly direction between two peaks of Mt Gamíla.

The villages in the vicinity of the gorge of Víkos are known as the Zagóri villages, or the Zagória, and are renowned for their strong traditional features.

To reach the gorge, take the Ioánnina-Kónitsa road and turn right towards the village of Monodéndri. This leads first through the picturesque village of Vítsa, and then to Monodéndri which lies on a high rise at the mouth of the Víkos gorge. Monodéndri has fine mansions, sturdy churches and picturesque little houses, all built of the local grey stone and surrounded with a profusion of greenery. It is one of the most

In the Víkos gorge.

The Voidomátis river, which has its source in the Víkos gorge.

traditional villages of Greece, and is being kept exactly as it was a hundred years ago. In the village square, which has an enormous plane tree, is a little restaurant which makes the famous Zagóri cheese pies *(tyrópittes).*

A small road leads through dense woodland to the side of the entrance to the gorge of Víkos and to the abandoned monastery of Aghía Paraskeví. From a raised terrace outside the monastery buildings one can see the beginning of the ravine hundreds of meters below. From the monastery, a path cut into the vertical mountain side leads to a cave where people used to hide in difficult times during the Turkish rule.

From Monodéndri there is a wide motor road which goes up to the so-called Víkos Balcony. The drive of approximately thirty minutes is through lush deciduous woodland and past large rocks which are fissured into horizontal layers, looking like tiles placed one on top of the other. The view from the Balcony is uniquely beautiful. It extends for almost the entire length of the gorge, with the Víkos river running down its centre, flanked by dense forest trees on either side.

To enter the gorge itself requires a steep descent on foot from Monodéndri village. At the bottom, the Mísios bridge spans the Víkos, and from here there is a half-obliterated path sometimes to the right, sometimes to the left of the river bed. The Víkos usually runs from October to June and dries up afterwards, making the journey somewhat easier. Both banks are guarded by thick green forest, and among the

The Víkos gorge as seen from the "Víkos Balcony" near Monodéndri village.

surrounding rocks are the many rare wild flowers and medicinal plants for which the gorge of the Víkos river has been famous for centuries.

A three-and-a-half hour walk up the valley arrives at the juncture of the Víkos gorge with the Méga Lákko ravine, which has a small cool stream running down it. After as much time again, the end of the gorge is reached, where the dried-up river bed suddenly becomes a proper river again up to 10 m wide and about a meter deep, fed by the Voïdomáti ("bull's eye") springs. Unfortunately, the place is deprived of much of its natural vegetation by the goats which graze here, stripping everything that grows and leaving only the plane trees.

From the springs one can either go up direct to the villages of Víkos or Pápingo, or take the at times difficult path along the river, past planes and willows, to the bridge on the road to Papingo, from where there is a bus service.

Mt Gamíla (or Týmphi, 2,497 m)

Mt Gamíla is both the most extensive and the most majestic of the Greek mountains. Its northern side consists of a range of cliffs about 15 km up from the valley of the Aóös river. These cliff faces, which are dissected by deep ravines and couloirs, are the reason this mountain has been compared to the Alps.

In contrast, the southern flanks of the mountain slope down gently to an extensive tableland. This, however, is abruptly cut off further down by the great gorge of the Víkos river and its tributaries.

Since this means that the mountain is almost completely surrounded by cliff faces, there are very few simple ascents to be made on foot. The classical way up is from the village of Pápingo on the western side of the mountain. This is reached by taking the road from Ioánnina to Kónitsa, which at one point veers right for a short climb up a hill. It then passes through the village of Arísti and afterwards drops down to the valley of the Voïdomátis river.

This is a truly charming place. In the background are the exit of the gorge of Víkos where the Voïdomátis has its crystal-clear spring, and that section of the Gamíla peak which is known as the Pýrgoi ("towers") of Pápingo because the mountain rises just above the village. All around is deep, green-filtered quiet, with willows and planes bending their branches towards the water as if listening to its murmured mountain stories.

From the Voïdomátis river, the road zig-zags up to Pápingo. The village is divided into Áno and Káto ("upper" and "lower") Pápingo, both of which have a small guesthouse. All the buildings are made of the local grey stone, and even the roofs have grey stone instead of clay tiles. Pápingo presents considerable historical interest, and had been declared a protected area where all construction of modern buildings is prohibited.

The ascent of Mt Gamíla from Pápingo presents no difficulty. If there is no snow it is easy to find the mountain hostel of the Greek Alpine Club of

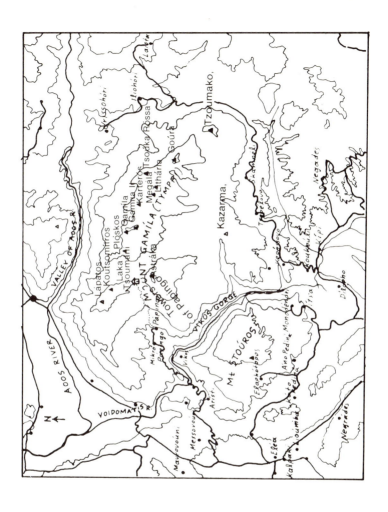

Map of Mt Gamíla with Aóos ravine and Víkos gorge.

The peaks of Mt Gamíla, seen from Mt Trapezitsa.

Ioánnina by going for two-and-a-half hours up an easy path with two springs along the way, keeping the great cliffs of the Pýrgoi of Pápingo always on the right.

The hostel has been built on a saddle between the peaks of Lápatos and Astráka. The entrance looks straight at the cliffs of Astráka, which provide opportunities for many worthwhile rock climbs. If a stay in the hostel is planned, where there are bunk beds, blankets and heating, this must be arranged beforehand with the Greek Alpine Club's offices in Ioánnina or with the authorised guard who lives in Pápingo village.

Astráka (2,436 m) is one peak of Mt Gamíla, others are Lápatos (2,251 m) further west which looms over the town of Kónitsa, and Koutsomítros (2,201 m) very close to Lápatos. Astráka, Lápatos and Koutsomítros stand rather seperated from the main peak line of the mountain, cut off by a valley with plenty of springs and lakes. All this water eventually joins the Aóös river, at a point not far from the monastery Moní Stomíou. The valley is known as Stáni tou Tsoumáni ("Tsoumáni's sheepfold"), after the family who graze their sheep here.

Other major peaks of Mt Gamíla are (west to east): Plóska (2,400 m), Gamíla (2,497 m), Gamíla II (2,480 m), Karterós (2,453 m), Megála Lithária (2,467 m), Tsoúka Róssa (2,377 m), Goúra (2,466 m), and Tzoumáko (2,157 m). For certain of these, the height given varies somewhat from one map to another.

Actually, each of the above peaks and its smaller satellites are mountains in their own right, and offer great mountaineering interest.

Many of the secondary peaks have vertical rockfaces on all sides and have never yet been climbed. In part, the reason for this is the brittle texture of the rock—which has not, however, deterred some of the most skilled of the Greek mountaineers from a great many rock climbs in the area. Ascents have also been made by some fine Italian climbers, as shown in the list of previous ascents given below.

From the Stáni Tsoumáni valley there is an uphill path along the edge of the Aóös valley west of the Plóska peak. This leads to a small but very deep lake, similar to that on Mt Smólika, which reflects in its waters the peaks of Plóska and Gamíla. This is the second of the two dragon lakes mentioned earlier in the chapter on mythology.

To go up to the summit of Mt Gamíla from the mountain hostel requires a descent into the Stáni Tsoumáni valley. From there an easterly turn leads across the plateau opposite. Keeping still in the same direction passes the south side of the foot of the Plóska peak, and arrives at the easy slope coming down from the top of Gamíla. From there a turn to the north leads to the summit.

The view is breathtaking: it feels as if one were suspended high above the chasm. Opposite lie the precipitous flanks of the Trapezítsa peak, covered with black and Balkan pines, below are the river and the green jungle of the ravine, and to the east, there is an almost unbroken line of mountain top upon mountain top.

Other routes to the summit of Mt Gamíla are from the villages of Vradéto, Tsepélovo, and Skamnélli south and south-east of the mountain.

Relatively easy paths from there traverse the great tablelands and end up at the top after four to five hours' walking.

From Skamnélli it is possible to go due north to the Goúra valley and from there to ascend the Goúra and Tsoúka Róssa peaks. The valley has a spring with plenty of clear water, and beautiful meadows for mountain camping.

The most difficult but also the most interesting route for non-climbers starts from Vrissohóri village. Passing below the northern cliffs of the Tsoúka Róssa, Megála Lithária and Karterós peaks, it comes out on the summit of Mt Gamíla via the Karterós saddle pass. This requires a trek of about ten hours' walking. The exact route is as follows.

Setting out from Vrissohóri village, a half-hour walk leads to the Boútsa spring, and a further half hour to Neraïdóvrissi ("neirads' spring"), close to the Dos-Yot gully. Fifteen minutes' walking from Neraïdóvrissi is Askitarió, a cave-like hollow in the rock. Two-and-a-half hours further on lies the small abandoned monastery of Aghiá Triáda, where water flows plentifully among lush greenery. Walking for another hour arrives at the Pixári spring, which is the last on the route for filling up water bottles.

From Pixári it is a two-hour climb to the Kaloyerikó saddle, and another hour's steep climbing past the Sádi Mígas cave opposite Bear Woods, to the Liméria ton Klephtón ("klephts' refuge"). Close-by, in the Tsiroyánni gully, is the Davéli cave. Another hour's climb comes out at the locality known as Kopána, which lies east of the Gamíla summit. Directly ahead is the Karterós pass, a couloir of scree which ends up at a pass of the same name between the mountains of Karterós and Gamíla. The climb up the scree to the pass takes about sixty to ninety minutes, and from there it needs about another hour to the summit of Gamíla.

This long but extremely beautiful ascent requires at least two days with an overnight stop on the way. Many mountaineers like to make it in early spring, when the snow adds extra interest, but also supposes a certain experience in winter climbing.

The Kopána locality is also used as a starting point for rock climbers attempting the surrounding peaks. Another such starting point for rock climbing or snow routes is the hostel of the Greek Alpine Club of Ioannina at the foot of the Astráka peak.

An interesting and worthwhile but difficult ascent of the peaks can be made from Moní Stomíou monastery in the Aóös valley. The path passes the points Exédra-Kerasiá-Amárandos-Daválitsa, and comes out in the Stáni Tsoumáni valley about six hours later.

An easterly branch-off from Exédra goes to the Kaloyeriká saddle where it joins up with another path coming from Vrissohóri.

PREVIOUS ASCENTS

Important rock climbs on the peaks of Mt Gamíla have been the following.

(1) *Tsoúka Róssa* First ascent of the vertical north-east face, 17 June 1955, by George Michaelídis, Michális Christodoúlou. 500 m, 11 hours. Very difficult.

Above: The Gamíla II peak seen from Gamila. *Below:* The Pýrgoi (towers) of Pápingo village.

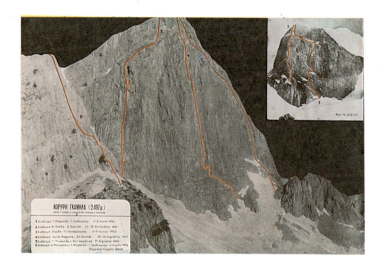

Some of the most important climbs on Gamila peak: 1. Michaelídis, Xanthópoulos, 7-8 June 1956—2. Idosídis, Tsantílis, 27-28 Sept. 1961.—3. Idosídis, Yiannakópoulos, 6-7 June 1963.—4. Magnone, Antípas, 25-26 Aug. 1960—5. Michaelídis, Deméstihas, 31 Aug. 1965.—6. Michaelídis, Xanthópoulos, 6 June 1956.

(2) *Gamíla* First ascent of vertical east face, 7-8 June 1956, by George Michaelídis, George Xanthópoulos. 450 m, 14 hours. Very difficult.

(3) *Gamíla* First ascent of vertical north-east face, 25-26 August 1960, by Guido Magnone, Spýros Antípas. 450 m, 12 hours. Very difficult.

(4) *Gamíla* First ascent of north edge, 27-28 September 1961, by Pródromos Idosídis, Dimítris Tsantílis. 450 m, 16 hours. Very difficult.

(5) *Gamíla* First ascent of vertical north-west face, 6-7 June 1963, by Pródromos Idosídis, P. Yannokópoulos. 550 m. Very difficult.

(6) *Gamíla* New route on the north edge, 7 August 1963, by M. Zephr, F. Galinós 400 m, 7 hours. Very difficult.

(7) *Mesoráhi* First of vertical north face, 6 June 1956, by George Michaelídis, George Xanthópoulos. Fairly difficult.

(8) *Pýrgos Pródromos* First ascent of the vertical north face, 24 April 1964. This ascent was the first ever of this peak, and the first attempt on the mountain in winter. It was made by Pródromos Idosídis, P. Yannakópoulos. 240 m, 12 hours. Very difficult.

(9) *Pýrgos 2440* First ascent of vertical north face, 5 October 1964, by Pródromos Idosídis, Dimitris Zafeirópoulos. 300 m, $5^{1}/_{2}$ hours. Difficult.

Drakólimni lake, with the Plóska or Plóskos peak on the right, and the Gamila peak in the distance.

The Lápatos peak on the left, rising above Kónitsa town, and Mt Grámmos in the distance.

(10) *Kalóyeros* First ascent of vertical north face, 6 October 1964, by Pródromos Idosídis, Dimítris Zafeirópoulos. 130 m, 2 hours. Medium difficult.

(11) *Pýrgos Gámma 1* First ascent of north-west edge by Bianca di Beaco, Walter Mejak.

(12) *Peak 30 October Trieste* First ascent of vertical north-west face, and first ascent of the peak ever, 5 July 1969, by Sergio Glavina, Franco d' Urso. Difficult. Grade 4 to 4+.

(13) *Pýrgos Gámma 3* First ascent by north couloir, July 1969, by Franco d'Urso, Sergio Glavina. 1 hour. Easy. Grade 2 and 3.

(14) *Pýrgos Gámma 3* First ascent of south ridge with a third-grade pass, July 1969, by Franco d'Urso, Sergio Glavina.

The small lakes in the Lákka tou Tsoumáni valley, and the Astráka peak in the distance. About the middle of the vertical mountain face is the "Edge of the Triesters".

(15) *Gamíla 2* First ascent of vertical west face, July 1962, by Virgilio Zecchini, Spíro dalla Porta-Xidias. 300 m, 4¹/₂ hours. Medium difficult. Grade 3+ to 3.

(16) *Tsoúka Róssa* First ascent by the couloir second from the left of the north-east peak of the group, 12 August 1966, by D. Liángos, G. Tsamakídis. 650 m, 5 hours. Medium difficult.

(17) *Peak 30 October Trieste* First ascent of vertical east face, 5 July 1969, by Bianca di Beàco, Walter Mejak. 350 m, 1 hour. Easy. Grade 2.

(18) *Kodonostásio (Gámma 9)* First ascent of north-east ridge, and first ascent ever of this peak, July 1969, by Sergio Glavina, Franco d'Urso. 30 minutes. Easy. Grade 2.

(19) *Pýrgos Gámma 11* First ascent of north edge, July 1969, by Virgilio

The north and north-east faces of Astráka. In the lower part of the picture, the Astráka saddle and the mountain hostel.

Zecchini, Spíro dalla Porta-Xidias. 320 m, 5 hours. Difficult, Grade 5 and 6.

(20) *Pýrgos Gámma 10* First ascent of south-west face, and first ascent ever, July 1962, by Bianca di Beaco, Walter Mejak. 200 m Medium difficult. Grade 4.

(21) *Pýrgos Gámma 12* First ascent of north-east edge, July 1969, by Bianca di Beaco, Walter Mejak. 400 m, 2 hours. Medium difficult. Grades 2 to 4.

(22) *Astráka* First route along north edge, summer 1965, by Virgilio Zecchini, Spiro dalla Porta-Xidias. 600 m. Very difficult. Grade 6. Since then it has been called "Edge of the Triesters".

(23) *Astráka* New route on north-north-west face, August 1977, by Flavio Ghio, George Martzoúkos. 550 m, $3^1/_2$ hours. Difficult. Grade 4.

The north and north-west faces of Astráka.

(24) *Astráka* First winter ascent of north-north-west face, 24 December 1974, by Dimitris Korrés Dimitris Haïtóglou, Bábbis Annousás, Katerina Gékka, who named the route "Couloir of Democracy". 350 m, 11 hours. Difficult.

(25) *Astráka* First winter ascent by the left-hand couloir on the north-west side, 26 March 1959, by George Michaelídis, Leóntios Leontiádis, Max Paraskevaídis.

(26) *Astráka* First winter ascent on couloir on the west side, Easter 1972, by George Sfíkas, Leftéris Tirópoulos, Gogó Moutsópoulos, Dimítris Panayotákos, Ersi Korónis, Maria Vasileádou, I. Papakonstantínou.

(27) *Pýrgoi Pápingou-Pýrgos Koúpas* First ascent of west face, 30-31

The Tsoúka Róssa peak of Mt Gamíla, above Vrissohóri village.

Mt Vasilítsa, southwest of Mt Smólikas

May 1965, by Pródromos Idosídis, Nikos Kotziás. 720 m, 17 hours. Difficult.

(28) *Pýrgoi Pápingou-Pýrgos Ptinó* First ascent of west face, 1 June 1965, by Pródromos Idosídis, Nikos Kotziás 500 m, 12 hours. Difficult.

Mt Vasilítsa (2,249 m)

Mt Vasilítsa lies south-east of Mt Smólikas. The ascent to the summit begins at the village of Avdéla, west of the town of Grevená and connected to it by a fairly good road. Avdéla has almost no permanent residents left today, but in the summer months fills up with holiday makers. There is a taverna as well as a guesthouse.

The path up in the mountain starts from the village square. At first it climbs over several sparsely treed hills and eventually comes out on the bare mountain. Mt Vasilítsa is mostly an earth mountain, not rocky, and has reddish soil.

The path finally leads to a goat pen where there are a number of fierce guard dogs, and from there to the base of the conical summit, where there is another such pen with a spring and more of the very unsociable large

Church near Perivóli village. (Photo J. Syrópoulos)

dogs. It is advisable to walk in a tight group and have at least a big stick for emergencies.

Altogether, the trek from Avdéla to the summit is four to five hours. Along the approach to the triangular point grow various alpine plants, among them the very rare wild violets *Viola brachyphylla, V. dukadjinica* and *V. magellensis.*

There is a superb view from the top. In the background rests the sturdy mass of Mt Smólikas, and in the west the characteristic tip of the summit of Mt Gamíla can be seen.

The return is either along the same way, or towards Samarína village. And again proper respect must be shown to the enormous dogs which are not in the least amused by playful or friendly advances.

Mt Lígkos (or East Píndus, 2,177 m)

This mountain, which is also known as simply the East Pindus, lies north-west of the village Miliá of Métsovon. Its peaks form a ring round the famous valley of Vália Kálda. They are peak Avgó (2,777 m) and Pyrostiá (1967) to the north; Aftiá (2,075 m), Phlégka (2,159 m),

Church in Samarína village, one of the largest of the triple-aisled basilicas of the Pindus region. The church is justly famous for its carved wooden altar screen, but is known also for the black pine which has planted itself on the roof.

Mavrovoúni (2,050 m) in the south, lying in a straight line from west to east; and closing the ring is the peak Miliá (2,160 m) which joins up from the east.

To climb up to these various peaks of Mt Lígkos, start by car or local bus from Métsovo, taking the road to Thessalian Tríkala. (Greece has several towns called Tríkala, hence the qualification.) At a place called Kámbos tou Despóti ("field of the despot") take the forest road which runs north to the village of Miliá. The residents here are mostly woodcutters. There is no guesthouse, but the inhabitants will gladly provide a bed for the night.

If it is not raining next morning, and if a private car is being used, take the forest road to the Vália Kálda valley. The route runs almost uninterruptedly through beautiful stands of Scots pine *(Pinus silvestris)* which is rare in Greece.

The Vália Kálda is the source of one of the tributaries of the Aóös river, and this stream tumbles down the middle of the valley, gurgling and bubbling merrily. From here, continue either north along the forest road to the villages of Perivóli and Avdéla, or use the valley as a base camp for ascents up the surrounding peaks. The latter absolutely require a guide from the village, since it is very easy indeed to get lost in the dense forest.

Above: On Mt Lígkos, near the Miliá peak. *Below:* Trees in the Vália Kálda valley.

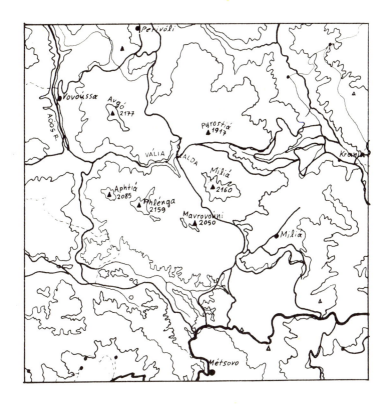

Map of Mt Lígkos, or the Eastern Pindus.

SOUTHERN PINDUS RANGE

Mt Peristéri of Métsovon (2,295 m)

Mt Peristéri lies south of Métsovo and is the most northerly of the mountains in the Southern Pindus range. There is another mountain of the same name on the Greek-Yugoslav border, the summit of which is on Yugoslav territory.

To climb Mt Peristéri of Métsovo, it is best to have spent the night in Métsovo (having come from Ioánnina or Thessalian Tríkala the day before), and to begin the ascent by driving to the village of Anthohóri south-west of Métsovo.

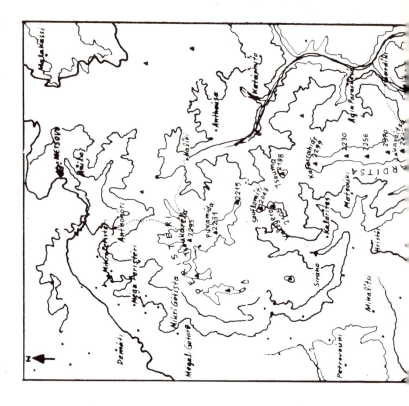

This is the start of a footpath through the valley, with various rocky peaks to the right and the left. The place is bare of trees almost right from the start. An approximately four-hour walk arrives at the foot of the highest peak (Tsoukarélla) and another hour or so is required to reach the conical summit.

The descent can be made by either returning along the same route, or by going down towards Halíki village.

Mt Kakardítsa (2,429 m)

Mt Kakardítsa is the highest mountain in the Southern Pindus. It consists of a long narrow line of peaks running north to south, and

Map of the north section of the Southern Pindus, with Mts Peristéri, Kakardítsa and Tsoumérka, which form a continuous chain.

connects up in the north with Mt Peristéri of Métsovon, and in the south-west with the peakline of Mt Tsoumérka. In fact, Mt Kakardítsa is often confused with Mt Tsoumérka, and on many maps the two are listed as one.

The conical summit of Mt Kakardítsa lies west of the village of Gardíki, where the shortest of the ascent routes starts, taking approximately four hours. Another route, which takes longer but goes up more gradually, begins from the village of Neráïda south of the mountain. From there, a roughly five-hour march comes out on a plateau from which the summit cone is clearly visible to the east. Descending first to a pass, and from there climbing up to the summit requires about another hour.

The descent will have to be made towards Gardíki village because returning to Neráïda takes too long to be accomplished for certain before nightfall.

Winter ascent of Mt Peristéri.

The Métsovo monastery, and snowy Mt Peristéri in the background.

Mt Tsoumérka (or Athamaniká Óri, 2,393 m)

Although Mts Kakardítsa and Tsoumérka are frequently considered as one, this is a mistake since the two mountains are quite clearly seperated by an obvious enough division, known as the pass of Melissourgoí. The secondary name of Athamaniká Óri for the two mountains together is also incorrect in that it is obsolete; though it was used in antiquity, none of the local people nowadays knows what it is supposed to refer to.

A relatively easy ascent of Mt Tsoumérka, taking four to five hours, can be made from the village of Thodóriana. The path starts out by following a treeless gully near Thodóriana, and arrives on the large plateau known as Kostelláta. From there it ascends the mountain side towards the summit peak, which is called Kataphídi. The last part of the route is over the rocks of a precipitous ridge, both sides of which fall away very steeply.

From the top, the view to the west shows the village Katarraktis and other, smaller hamlets. To the north lie the massifs of Peristéri and Kakardítsa, to the east is Mt Hatzí and smaller mountains, and the south is dominated by the peaks of the Ágrapha range. Among the rocks grow many kinds of wild flowers, the different colours of which are the only gentle note in the otherwise harsh and wild surroundings.

The return route goes back to Thodóriana, or down to Drosopygí village (formerly Voulgaréli).

If the ascent is made from Drosopygí it takes about half as long again—approximately six hours. At first the route climbs above the village through fir woods until it comes out on the bare mountain. Continuing between the peaks 2087 and 1932, it emerges later on almost level ground. Eventually the Kostelláta plateau is reached, from where the route continues uphill to the left towards the Kataphídi summit.

There is yet another way up, and this is clearly marked with patches of colour on the trees etc. It starts from the village of Katarraktis east of the mountain, and is quicker than either of the other two but much steeper.

It is worth mentioning that Tsoumérka is a mountain plentifully supplied with water. There are small streams everywhere which form a lively contrast to the stark, rocky surroundings. There are even two fine waterfalls in this area. One of them is close to Katarraktis village, and the other near Thodóriana. They are well worth a detour.

Mt Kóziakas (1,901 m)

To the west of Thessalian Tríkala is a mountain with a rather intricately broken-up summit. This is Mt Kóziakas, which rises quite abruptly from the plain of Thessaly.

To get to the top, take the road for Pýli village (formerly known as Pórta), where there are two stops worth making: to visit the Byzantine church of Pórta Panayiá, and to look at the arched bridge over the Portaïkós river, which starts high up in the mountains and rushes down a very steep ravine which is like a door from the Pindus range to the plain.

After Pýli the road twists uphill and eventually arrives at Eláti village (formerly Tírna) on the western flank of Mt Kóziakas. This is a well-kept place with something of a tourist trade. There are small hotels, many houses where rooms can be rented, and two or three restaurants. With the abrupt height of Mt Kóziakas towering above, Eláti is reminiscent of villages in Switzerland.

With Eláti as the starting point, the actual ascent of the mountain can begin the next morning. Five kilometers down the forest road to Pertoúli begins a well-defined path which leads to the hostel of the Educational Excursion Club of Tríkala. The highest peak of Mt Kóziakas is straight above the hostel of the east. Just next to the building there is a spring.

Mt Kóziakas is very rocky, with only the sparsest tree cover on its higher reaches, though it is densely forested lower down. On its western flanks is one of the most beautiful stands of fir anywhere in Greece, and this spreads right across to the slopes of Mt Avgó opposite. This is the famous Pertoúli Forest, the timber resources of which are most carefully husbanded by the authorities.

From the summit of Mt Kóziakas, the great plain of Thessaly is seen to spread out towards the east, and to the west is the peakline of Mt Avgó, with the peaks of Loupáta and Maróssa, and Avgó itself. Farther north-west rise the proud summits of Mts Tsoumérka and Kakardítsa.

Top left: The waterfall near Thodóriana village. *Top right:* Melissourgoí village and Mt Tsoumérka in the distance. *Below:* Church in Melissourgoí. (All three photos by J. Sotirópoulos)

Left: On the summit line of Mt Kóziakas. *Right* Approach to the Maróssa peak in the Avgó massif.

Mt Avgó of the Southern Pindus (2,148 m)

Mt Avgó ("the egg") of the Southern Pindus must not be confused with the other Mt Avgó which is one of the peaks of the large Mt Lígkos group in the Northern Pindus. The summit ridge of the (southern) mountain culminates in three major peaks: Loupáta, Maróssa, and Avgó, which is the highest.

The most interesting of these three is the steep rocky cone of Maróssa. The ascent route starts from the village of Neraïdohóri, which is reached from Tríkala via Eláti and Pertoúli. From Neraïdohóri, it continues through fairytale fir woods, later comes out on a bare open place, and continues at an easy climb to one of the lesser peaks. From this, access to Maróssa is via a difficult rocky ridge. This cannot be avoided since all the other sides of Maróssa are vertical, leaving no alternative route.

From the Maróssa peak the much more regular summit of Mt Avgó can be reached by continuing westwards.

The descent from Mt Avgó is towards the village of Pýrra, down easy slopes to a spring, from which there is a path which leads all the way to the

Mt Avgó as seen from Mt Kóziakas. From left to right: peaks Loupáta, Maróssa and Avgó.

village. There is only one obstacle on the way: a river, luckily a shallow one, which needs to be forded.

The ascent of Mt Avgó can, of course, be made straight from Pýrra village.

The Ágrapha range (2,164 m)

What is also known simply as Mt Ágrapha is in fact a complex mountain range in the Southern Pindus, including dozens of mountains both large

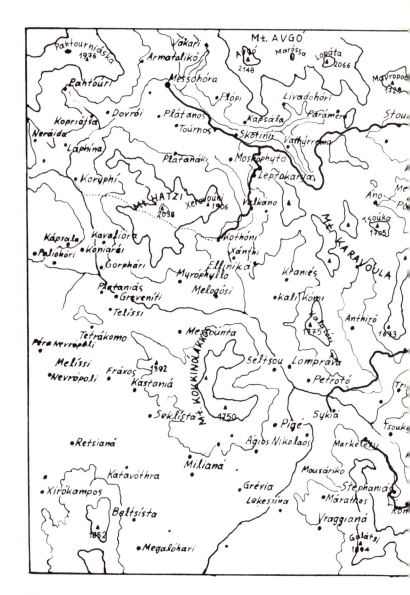

Map of part of Southern Pindus, showing the northern section of the Ágrapha range with Mts Kokkinólakos, Karavotla Karáva, Voutsikáki and Delidími, as well as the independent heights of Mts Hatzí, Avgó Kóziakas.

The Borléro peak in the Eastern Ágrapha massif.

and small and a number of clearly defined peaks. The northernmost mountain in the Ágrapha range, south of Mt Kóziakas, is Karavoúla (1,862 m). To the south of Karavoúla peak is Karáva (2,128 m), and to the east of that lies peak Kazárma (1,971 m). South of Kazárma is the peak of Voutsikáki (2,154 m), from which the range forks southwards.

The western ridge culminates in the peaks of Mt Delidími (2,164 m) which is the highest in all the Ágrapha range; Mt Phtéri with peaks Phtéri (2,128 m) and Liákoura (2,043 m) and other smaller mountains.

The other branch-off from peak Voutsikáki forms the eastern Ágrapha range, the main peaks of which are Svóni (2,042 m), Phlitzáni (2,018 m), Borléro (2,032 m), and Pláka (2,013 m). There is some unresolved

Left, peak Phlitzáni, and right, the Pláka peak in Eastern Ágrapha massif.

confusion about the names and heights of these peaks, as witnessed by several differences from one map to another.

Between the eastern and western ridges of the Ágrapha range, a number of mountain streams plunge down as torrents to form the Agraphiótis river, which in turn is responsible for the ravine of the same name. The sparkling waters of the Agraphiótis flow southwards and eventually join the Acheloós river.

A beautiful mountaineering excursion in the Ágrapha range can be made as set out below.

Starting by car from Kardítsa town on the plain of Thessaly, drive towards the mountains as far as the village of Kastaniá which is close to

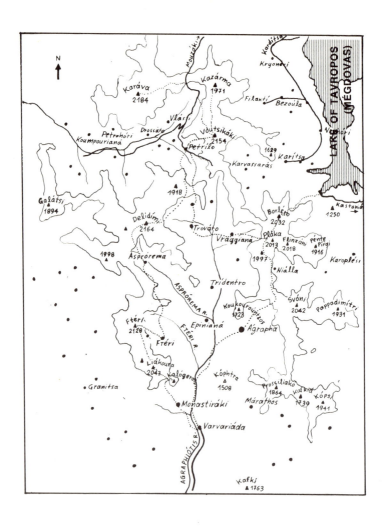

Map of the Ágrapha mountains, with the Agraphiótis river and the mountain paths.

The Agraphiótis river.

the man-made lake of Tavropós (Mégdovas). There is also a local bus to Kastaniá from Kardítsa. From the village, continue along a dirt road which goes as far as the enclosure of the lake, and then take a path which climbs towards the Borléro peak.

From above there is a delightful view of the lake ringed by the rich green of the fir forests. As the climb continues, the forest becomes increasingly less dense, until it has given place to open, mostly barren ground. There are occasional small clumps of beeches, and eventually the conical peak of Borléro appears in view directly ahead. All in all, the climb takes four to five hours.

The return can be made either along the same road, or down the opposite side along a good, though slightly longer path, towards the village of Ágrapha. This latter descent passes north of the peaks of Pláka

89

Hostel on Mt Veloúhi, at the Seïtáni locality.

and Phlitzáni, and then continues southwards, down through forests and ravines. This descent requires another five to six hours. It should be remembered to take the right-hand path at the fork about two hours from the peak, since the left-hand path provides unnecessarily exhausting obstacles.

Between the peaks of Borléro, Phlitzáni and Pláka are large tablelands suitable for summer mountain camping—either for its own sake, or as a base for ascents of the surrounding peaks. The peaks of Pláka and Phlitzáni are difficult and a challenge to rock climbers. From the camping sites one can go down to Ágrapha village, cross the ravine of the Agraphiótis river, and continue until meeting the road from Karpenísi and Agrinion.

A pleasant, part-motorised excursion to the peak of Voutsikáki can be made from the plain of Thessaly. Drive by car to Tríkala, from there to the village of Mouzáki and, still by car, to the little church of Ághios Nikólas where one can tent for the night. From here the ascent up the north side of Voutsikáki can be made, as also of the Kazárma peak next to it. Both these mountains can be climbed in one day, and the next day might be spent going up Mt Karáva.

Winter ascent of Mt Veloúhi. Many Greek mountaineers strip to the waist while climbing.

THE MOUNTAINS OF CENTRAL GREECE

Mt Veloúhi (or Tymphristós, 2,316 m)

Mt Veloúhi is in the very heart of Central Greece, north of the town of Karpenísi. It is a large mountain, but not very attractive aesthetically, since the major part of its forests has been destroyed.

The classical ascent starts along a good path from Karpenísi. The early part of the route goes past hills overgrown with shrubs and bushes. This is succeeded by a belt of fir trees , and for the rest of the way there is bare, open ground with little vegetation as far as the locality of Seïtáni, where at 1,840 m the Greek Alpine Club of Karpenísi has a hostel.

The same place can be reached by car, along a perfectly satisfactory dirt road. The area has become one of the best-organised ski centres in all of Greece. It has a small ski-lift and a number of very good beginners' slopes, as well as large ones for advanced skiers.

The hostel is about one hour's walk from the peak (if there is no snow).

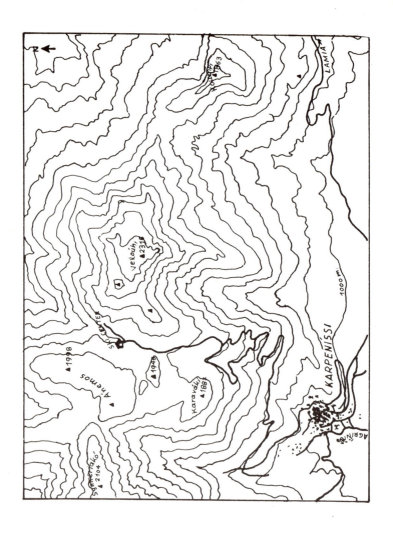

Map of Mt Veloúhi (Tymphristós), showing the highest peaks and the ski centre.

92

Mt Veloúhi seen from Mt Helidóna, the flanks of which are thickly wooded with Cephallonian fir.

Mt Helidóna seen from Mt Veloúhi.

Mt Helidóna (1,975 m)

A road from Karpenísi to the south follows the fast-running highland stream of Karpenisiótis until it arrives at Mikró Horió and Megálo Horió ("little" and "big village") which almost face each other across the river. Above the two villages loom Mts Helidóna and Kalliakoúda respectively.

To go up Helidóna, take the path starting from Mikró Horió and walk uphill in an easterly direction, passing through a valley of fir trees on the way. After about two hours the path comes out on the ridge, where another ninety minutes' climb to the south-west reaches at the summit.

Mt Kalliakoúda (2,101 m)

The starting point for the ascent of Mt Kalliakoúda is Megálo Horió (see above). The summer ascent (i.e. without snow) requires about four hours.

Take the well-defined path going east from the village, at first through fields, and later through stands of Cephallonian fir w hich alternate with pretty little meadow clearings. Where the forest ends, sheep pastures begin. The path finally comes to an end at the foot of the summit cone. At this point take a turn to the right, from where a continuous climb up a

The summit of Mt Kalliakoúda.

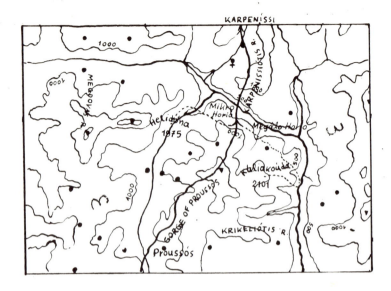

Map of Mts Helidóna and Kalliakoúda and environs.

rocky ridge finally ends up on the summit. This ridge is exceptionally difficult in winter and requires concentrated vigilance.

The view from the summit of Kalliakoúda is particularly impressive. In the west there is Mt Helidóna, and in the south the peaks of Panaitolikó, and many other lower but steep mountains stretch for miles in all directions. This is the heart of one of the most mountainous parts of Greece.

The descent is by the same route.

The gorge of Proussós

The road from Megálo Horió south to the village of Proussós traverses some very wild country: the Proussós gorge, which is a ravine formed by the Karpenisiótis river. Towering peaks, silently wooded and uncompromisingly bare, stand sentinel on every side. Further downstream, the Karpenisiótis meets up with the Krikeliótis, another small river which hurries down from the mountains to Kríkelo village, renowned since the resistance against the Germans in World War II.

The Proussós monastery lies to one side of the valley but is of no particular interest. Not much farther on, the road enters the village of Proussós, and from there it continues to Agrínion. It is possible to walk

The Pyramída peak of Mt Ghióna.

right down the length of the gorge of Proussós, but this requires the services of a local guide.

Mt Ghióna (2,510 m)

Mt Ghióna—or properly speaking the Pyramída peak of the Ghióna massif—is the highest point in Central Greece. It stands divided from the Vardoúsia mountains in the west by the Mórnos river. Its other neighbours are Mt Parnassós in the south-east, Mt Kallídromo in the north-east, and Mt Oíti in the north.

The main peaks are, in descending order of height: Pyramída (2,510 m), five unnamed peaks (2,496 m, 2,484, 2454, 2,453, and 2,404 m respectively), Platovoúna (2,319 m), Prophítis Ilías (2,301 m), Pyrgákia (2,198 m), Vráïla (2,176 m), Stállos (2,128 m), Koúkos (2,099 m), Pýrgos (2,066 m), Stenómandro (2,058 m), Koukoudiáris (2,055 m), Lyrítsa (2,041 m), Hioniás (1,993 m), and Devredés (1,974 m). For several peaks the height seems not to be absolutely certain, and there are differences from one map to another.

The classical ascent of the Pyramída summit peak begins from Kaloskopí village. To get there,take the Athens-Lamía national road, and

On Mt Ghióna, near the Mnímata locality.

after Thermopýlae turn left to Brállos. The road climbs and twists sharply as far as the pass seperating Mt Oíti from Mt Kallídromo. Shortly before Brállos there is a fork to the right for Pávliani, and in Pávliani there is a left turn for Kaloskopi.

From Kaloskopí it is possible to continue by car along the forest road to the place known as Mnímata ("memories"), from where the ascent of the Pyramída summit begins in earnest. About three hours' walking arrives at a plateau lying just below the rock mass of Pyramída. The ascent is made from the left-hand side facing the peak, and takes another ninety minutes or so.

An alternative route, longer and more tiring, goes up from the village of Lefkadíti. A third route, even longer, begins at the Rekká ravine.

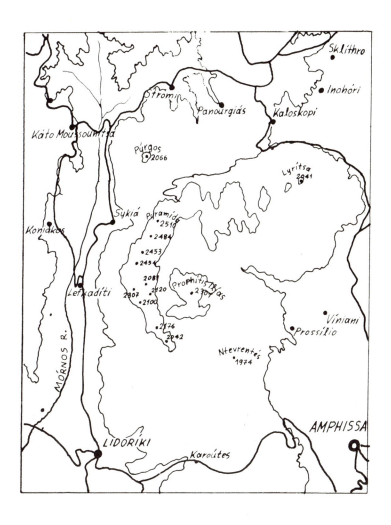

Map of Mt Ghióna and environs.

Spring ascent of the peaks of Mt Ghióna.

In the Ghióna mountains, above Sikiá village, is the famous Pláka cliff face, one of the highest cliffs in all of Greece. From the top of the Pláka cliff down to Sikiá it is a sheer drop of 12-13,000 m. Here, as on other vertical faces in the Ghióna massif, many notable rock climbs have been made, the most important of which are listed below.

PREVIOUS ASCENTS

(1) *Pyramída peak*   First ascent of west face, 8-9 June 1952, by Socrátes Lékkas, Yánnis Petróheilos, George Martzoúkos, Dimítris Boússios, Kaísaras Alexópoulos. 1,700 m, 18 hours. Medium difficult.

(2) *Pyramída peak.*   First ascent of north face, 1 May 1954, by George Michaelidis, Dimitris Liangos. 300 m, 7 hours.

(3) *Tsouknída peak*   First route up north-east face, 14 August 1955, by G. Michaelídis, G. Xanthópoulos. 300 m. 5$^{1}/_{2}$ hours. Difficult.

(4) *Pláka Sikiás*   First route up north-west face, 24 June 1959, by Noel Bloti, D. Liángos. 1,350 m, 14 hours. Difficult.

(5) *Pyramída peak*   Vertical north-north-west face, 25 July 1959, by Noel Bloti, G. Tsamakídis. 500 m. 7 hours. Very difficult.

(6) *Xerovouni peak.*   First ascent of east face, 1 August 1967 by J. Pantazidis. 250 m, 3 hours. Medium difficult.

Cliff face of Pláka near Sikiá village, with the five main routes mapped by climbers: I. G. Martzoúkos, S. Lékkas, D. Boússios I. Petróhilos, K. Alexópoulos.—2. R. Pillas, E. Tsakirákis, C. Stamatíou.—3. N. Nestgen, N. Karapatákis, D. Tsantílis.—4. G. Michaelídis, L. Leontiádis, M. Paraskevaídis.—5. G Michaelídis, Kétty Michaelídou, E. Maidos, S. Hatziloukás, P. Bakális, B. Giátsios. (Photo J. Prokopíou)

Aráhova village, with the Mt Parnassós peaks in the background.

Mt Parnassós (2,457 m)

The highest point in the mass of Mt Parnassós is the Liákoura peak (2,457 m). The classical ascent of this starts out from the Sarandári site where the Greek Alpine Club of Athens has a hostel at 1,900 m elevation. A very good road comes as far as this from Aráchova, and then continues to the ski centre of Phterólakka and from there drops down to Amphíklia village.

Very near the Greek Alpine Club hostel is a ski centre run by the Athens Skilovers' Club. The nearest neighbouring peak is Yerontóvrahos (2,367 m) which can be climbed in about ninety minutes.

Other peaks of Mt Parnassós more than 2,000 m high are: Kotróni (2,428 m), Tsárkos (2,414 m), the 2409, 2393 and 2376 peaks Mávra

The Yerontóvrahos peak of Mt Parnassós. *Overleaf:* Map of Mt Parnassós.

Lithária or Trípa (2,334 m), Raïdólakka (2,328 m), Énneza (2,328 m), Arnóvrissi (2,257 m), Sési (2,120 m), and Koúkos (2,112 m).

To climb to the Liákoura summit from the Greek Alpine Club hostel requires going round the north side of Yerontóvrahos. The up-and-down route over hills and plateaus finally arrives at the foot of the summit. The incline is gradual, and the ascent from this point easy. Walking time from the hostel is around three to four hours.

Another route up Mt Liákoura, much more difficult but also more interesting from a mountaineering point of view, can be made with the village of Áno Tithoraía (formerly Velítsa) to start out from, and then through the Velítsa ravine. This is the side of Mt Parnassós which shows all the wild grandeur of the mountain to perfection. The ascent to the Liákoura summit takes around six hours and becomes more difficult nearer the top as the angle of the slope steepens.

The ascent of Mt Parnassós can, of course, be combined with a visit to the famous temple at Delphí on the flanks of the mountain. This route would start from the village of Aráchova very early in the morning, and definitely requires a guide.

The many sheer peaks and cliff faces of Parnassós offer interesting rock climbs. The most important made to date are given below.

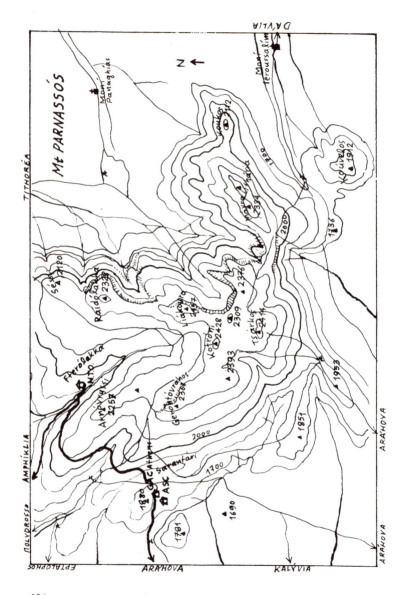

Mt PARNASSÓS

N

104

Walking through the splendid woods of Mt Oíti.

PREVIOUS ASCENTS

(1) *Yerontóvrahos peak*   First ascent of north-east face, 30 June 1950, by N. Damías, K. Alexópoulos. 230 m, $4^1/_2$ hours. Generally Grade 3.

(2) *Yerontóvrahos peak*   Route up north-west face, 12 October 1958, by Stávros Píssalas, Michális Christodoúlou. 210 m, $2^1/_2$ hours. Grade 3-4

(3) *Yerontóvrahos peak*   Route up north-west face, 2 November 1958, by C. Stamatíou, L. Leontiádis. 150 m, 2 hours. Grade 3.

(4) *Koúvelos peak*   Route up south face, 20 May 1962, by G. Michaelídis, Ilias Trohánis. Grade 4-5.

(5) *Koúkos peak*   First ascent of north-east face, 13-14 June 1954, by G. Michaelídis, Anna Petróheilos, D. Mángos, G. Tsamakídis. 1,000 m, 15 hours.

Mt Oíti (2,152 m)

Mt Oíti (or Oeta in English texts telling of the death of Hercules—see chapter on mythology) is one of the most beautiful of Greece's mountains, covered with splendid woods of Greek fir or, where there are no trees, soft meadows studded with rare wild flowers.

Mt Oíti straddles two prefectures, Phthiótida and Phokída; the nearest town to it is Lamía. To the south it is bounded by the Ghióna massif, in the

The hostel on Mt Oíti in winter.

east by Mt Kallídromo, and in the west by the Vardoúsia mountains. Its
northern flanks drop sharply down to the valley of the Sperchiós river.

The summit of this mountain is called Pýrgos (2,152 m). All around
Pýrgos ("tower") lie other peaks, forming a vast interconnected
mountain group. Alíkaina (2,058 m) is to the north, 2,600 m away as the
crow flies, and Pyrá 1,250 m to the south-west; Phterotós lies south-west
2,400 m away, and Sémbi peak (2,093 m) is 1,300 m off to the north-east.
Other peaks rather farther away from Pýrgos are Xerovoúni (1,789 m)
above the village of Pávliani, and Aitós (1,704 m) above the village of
Kastaniá. Standing further apart still in the distance is the Grevenó peak
(2,116 m), lying north-east of the Pýrgos summit and seperated from the
main Oíti group by the Livadiés ("meadows") tableland.

On the Grevenó peak of Mt Oíti, with other peaks in the distance.

The classic route to the top starts from Ypáti village. In the middle ages Ypáti was the capital town of a duchy, and was then known as Néai Pátrai; during the Turkish occupation it became Patratzíki. The path starts from the highest point in the village, and after an hour's walking over bare ground enters a fir forest. After another 15 minutes it arrives at a small meadow with an enclosure for sheep and fresh water. It then ascends among fir trees, and ninety minutes later reaches the Amalióvrissi spring. Shortly after this there is a meadow, and instead of continuing straight on, the route goes down to the right into a gully and uphill again through lovely forest as far as the Perdikóvrissi spring. The distance between the two springs is about thirty minutes. After another forty-five munutes through forest, the small Trápeza plateau is reached, where at 1,800 m there is a hostel of the Greek Alpine Club of Lamía.

The view from the hostel is magnificent. In the evening, the village lights twinkle down on the Lamía plain as far as the eye can see. To the east looms the rocky mass of peak Grevenó, on this side dropping vertically down into the ravine which separates it from the hostel.

The hostel can also be reached by a dirt road through the forest from the village of Kastaniá, but this is passable by car only in summer, and the car needs to be a robust one even then.

Continuing the ascent, take the forest road from the hostel, passing through a rocky defile and coming out in the Livadiés tableland, where there are two small lakes. North of the tableland lies the Grevenó peak, the summit of which is about ninety minutes away. It offers a wonderful view of the surrounding mountains—Parnassós, Ghióna, Vardoúsia etc.

For the top of the Pýrgos summit, go west from the Livadiés tableland to start with, and then south, up the symmetrically-shaped peak.

The descent can be made to another spring also called Perdikóvrissi, and then towards the villages of Pyrrá or Mavrolithári.

On the Livadiés tableland is the source of a little river, the Valórema, which has cut a deep gully on its way down to the plain of Lamía. Further downstream it changes name and becomes the Gorgopótamos. The bridge over the Gorgopótamos is famous in guerrilla history, for having been blown up in World War II by Greek resistance fighters and English saboteurs, infiltrated to help them.

The Livadiés tableland can also be reached by car or on foot from the village of Pávliani, cutting across the entire mountain in a north-westerly direction along a forest road which goes round the Xerovoúni peak. When it arrives at the site of Katavóthra ("deep hole"), a cave will be found at the foot of a vertical cliff, and deep inside it there is water. This is also the end of the footpath from Pávliani, which is rather shorter because it avoids the long detour all around Xerovoúni.

Continuing either by car or on foot, take the dirt road through very beautiful forest. A little after Katavóthra it arrives at a place called Tirokomío, where on the left of the road a large spring bubbles straight out of the rock. Later there are shepherds' huts on the right, at a locality called Matákia. Later still the road passes Valórema and starts the final climb to the Livadiés tableland. On foot, the above route takes about $5^1/_2$ hours, by car about two hours.

The Vardoúsia mountains (2,495 m)

From the mountaineer's point of view, the Vardoúsia range is one of the most exciting areas in the Greek mountains. Its dozens of peaks, bare and precipitous, exert a strong pull and demand to be climbed. Many of them

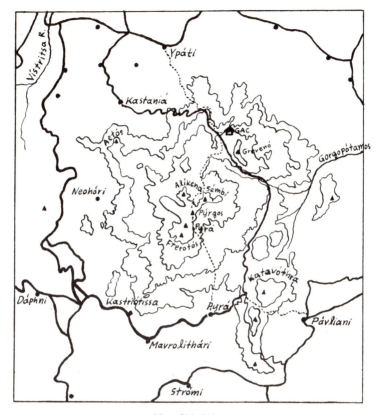

Map of Mt Oíti.

are accessible only to rock climbers, but all, even the easiest routes, present plenty of difficulties, which are of course exacerbated in winter.

The Vardoúsia mountains divide into three main groups of peaks. The northern group is characterised by peaks with regular flanks their eastern side, and precipitous scarps in the west, which include the clifl known as Méga Zástano. The two highest peaks in this group are Sinánı (2,059 m) in the north, and the unnamed 2286 in the south.

The southern group lies in a continuous long narrow mass running from north to south. It begins above the village of Áno Moussounítsa and ends at Stenó village not far from Lidoríki. The highest peak in this group is Kórakas (2,495 m). South of Kórakas are the peaks 2414, Kokkiniàs (2,406 m), 2322, 2240, 2220, 2080 and others, and to its north yet another

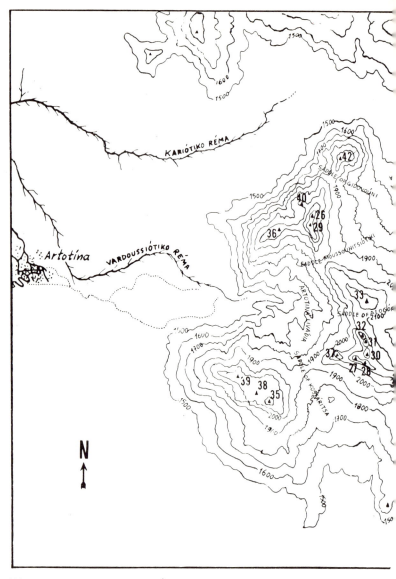

KARIÓTIKO RÉMA

Artotína

VARDOUSSIÓTIKO RÉMA

SADDLE OF GIDOVOÚNI

SADDLE OF MOUSSOUNÍTSIOTIKI

ARTOTINÁ LIVÁDIA

SADDLE OF PYRGOS

SADDLE OF KOKKORÍTSA

42

40

26
29

36

33

32
31

34

30

27 28

39

38

35

N

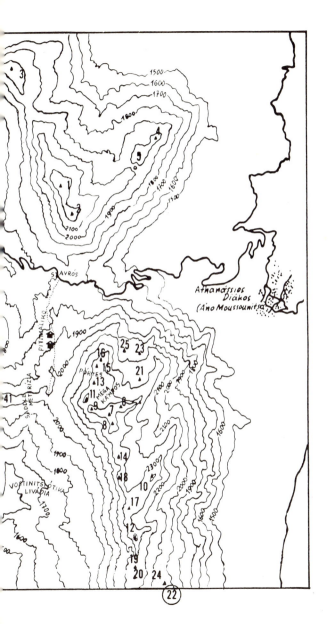

Map of the Vardoússia mountains and their environs. On the following page, a list of the peaks by name and height.

111

TABLE OF VARDOUSSIA PEAKS
Northern Group

1	Unnamed	2,286 m
2	Unnamed	2,2.. m
3	Sinani	2,059 m
4	Unnamed	2,020 m
5	Unnamed	2,... m

Southern Group

6	Kórakas or Ai Lias	2,495 m
7	Unnamed	2,46. m
8	Unnamed	2,46. m
9	Unnamed	2,437 m
10	Kókkini Tsouma	2,414 m
11	Aitós	2,41. m
12	Kokkinias	2,406 m
13	Liontari	2,38. m
14	Unnamed	2,38. m
15	Skórda Pitimalikou I	2,38. m
16	Skórda Pitimalikou II	2,38. m
17	Unnamed	2,36. m
18	Unnamed	2,322 m
19	Unnamed	2,240 m
20	Unnamed	2,220 m
21	Dónti tou Kóraka	2,160 m
22	Unnamed	2,080 m
23	Unnamed	2,060 m
24	Klissoura	2,040 m
25	Tou Gióni tó Plai	2,040 m

Western Group

26	Pyramida	2,350 m
27	Kentriki Soufla or Dihala	2,34. m
28	Anatoliki (east) Soufla	2,34. m
29	Plaka Pyramidas	2,32. m
30	Vória (North) Soufla I	2,3.. m
31	Vória (North) Soufla II	2,3.. m
32	Vória (North) Soufla III	2,3.. m
33	Alogórrahi	2,270 m
34	Unnamed Soufla	2,26. m
35	Vounó Kostaritsas I	2,256 m
36	Kato Psiló	2,22. m
37	Ditiki (West) Soufla	2,2.. m
38	Vounó Kostaritsas II	2,18. m
39	Vounó Kostaritsas III	2,16. m
40	Pano Psiló	2,16. m
41	Meterizia	2,058 m
42	Gidovouni	2,037 m
43	Plaka Vostinitsas I	1,948 m
44	Plaka Vostinitsas II	1,840 m

It should be noted that the Soufles group of peaks is also known under the general name of Plaka, which is entirely incorrect. Furthermore, certain maps give the overall name of Kórakas for the group of peaks Gidovouni, Pyramida, Plaka Pyramidas, Pano Psiló, and Kato Psiló. This too is misleading, since there is no doubt that Kórakas is the highest mountain in the southern group.

Winter on the Kórakas peak, with the ice-capped altimeter on the left.

unnamed peak with a long ridge. Its height has not been established, and
very few mountaineers have visited it. To its north and north-west lie
other unnamed peaks. West of Kórakas is peak 2437.

- Between the southern and northern groups of the Vardoúsia
mountains, and west of Áno Moussounítsa village is a saddle. The area
here is called Stavrós ("cross"). The third, the western group is seperated
from the northern by the Moussounitsiótika meadows and the small
Évinnos mountain stream. Between the western and the southern group
lie the sloping meadows known as Pittimáliko, and the Meterízia pass.

The western group is the most interesting of the three. It consists of a
series of very steep peaks separated by high passes. In the north is the
Gidovoúni peak (2,037 m), the southern side of which forms sheer cliffs
dropping down to the Gidovoúni saddle. The next peak further south is

113

Peak Liontári, with the Soúfles peaks beyond, seen from the Mega Kámbos tableland.

Pyramída (2,350 m), followed by the slightly lower Pláka Pyramídas, the eastern face of which is a big vertical cliff.

North-west of Pyramída lies the famous peak of Páno Psiló (2,140 m). Pyramída and Páno Psiló are joined by the Pórta pass, from which the ascent of Páno Psiló is easy. The west face of Páno Psiló, on the other hand, presents one of the largest of the Greek mountain cliffs, made of solid rock, which has only once been climbed, by two Greek mountaineers.

Another impressive peak of the Vardoúsia mountains is Káto Psiló, which the local shepherds often call Apátiti. It is the only one in this range where even the normal route requires fairly difficult rock climbing with

The Pláka Vostinítsas peak on the left, the Meterízia saddle at left bottom and the Soúfles group in the middle. The photo was taken from the Pórtes location on Kórakas peak.

ropes. So far, there have been very few ascents. Káto Psiló is seperated from the bulk of Pyramída by the Káto Psiló saddle.

South of Pláka Pyramídas is what is known as the Moussounitsiótiki saddle, beyond which to the south lies peak Alogórahi (2,270 m), relatively the easiest of the western group. Further south still is the Laimós ("neck") tis Alogórahis saddle, which divides the peak of the same name from the mass known as Soúfles. This is made up of five rocky and pointed peaks, the centre one of which is split down the middle and looks like a two-pronged fork. It is also the highest of the five, and is known as Kentrikí Soúfla (2,260 m) and is the only Soúfles peak of which the height has been established. Of the remaining four, West Soúfla and

115

East Soúfla have a great deal of character, but the other two are rather lower and relatively less distinguished. The entire group has precipitous cliffs, and on some of these, interesting rock climbing has been done.

Yet another fine peak is Pláka Vostinítsas (1,948 m), the east side of which, unbeknownst to most Greek mountaineers, forms a steep cliff. Finally, west of the Soúfles group lies the peak Vounó tis Kostáritsas (2,256 m), on the other side of the Kostaritsas pass.

The peaks of Káto Psiló, Pyramída, Pláka Pyramídas, Alogórahi, the Soúfles and Vounó tis Kostáritsas form a semicircle around the Artotiná meadows, and south of the Meterízia saddle and east of peak Pláka Vostinítsa are the Vostinitsiótika meadows.

The usual ascent of the Vardoúsia mountains begins from the village of Áno Moussounítsa towards the locality of Pittimáliko, where the Greek Alpine Club of Lamía and the Athens Hiking Club have hostels for 15-18 persons each. The walk to the hostels takes around $3^1/_2$ hours if there is no snow. There is also a forest road to Moussounítsa from Stavrós, but cars can only use it in summer, and even then not for sure. The hostels are one hour from Stavrós.

With either of the two hostels as a base, all the surrounding peaks can be climbed. The ascent of Kórakas, the summit peak, goes through a couloir as far as the site of Pórtes. Continuing from here, the route comes out on the tableland of Méga Kámbos, at the edge of which stands the cone of Kórakas. Without snow the ascent takes around three hours. The other side of Kórakas can be climbed from the villages of Áno Moussounítsa, Koniákos, and Diakópi as starting points.

For the peaks of the western group, the ascent is made from the west, from Artotina village, ending up at the Artotiná meadows where camp can be set up. From here, new expeditions can be made every day.

The Vardoúsia range is of exceptional interest to rock climbers. It has a large number of cliffs of varying grades, some of them very difficult. The list below gives some of the more important previous ascents.

PREVIOUS ASCENTS

(1) *Skórda* First ascent of west cliff, Easter 1951, by George Michaelídis, Godefrid Polykrátis, Stélios Vasilópoulos. 300 m. Medium difficult.

(2) *Skórda* Two new routes up the west cliff, 13 August 1958, by George Michaelídis and Spýros Antípas; and by George Tsamakídis and Pétros Semitákis. 250 m. Difficult.

The previous pages show the Vardoúsia peaks (left to right) Alogórahi, Pláka, Pyramída, and Gidovoúni.

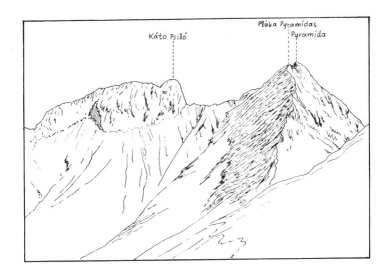

The Vardousia peaks of Kato Psiló, Pyramída, and Pláka Pyramídas, seen from the west side of the Alogórahi peak.

(3) *Skórda* First ascent of west cliff of south peak (Skórda Pittimálikou), 13 August 1958, by Dimítris Liángos, Maria Ioánnou. 200 m. Difficult.

(4) *Dónti tou Kóraka* First ascent up north-east face, 1 June 1958, by G. Michaelídis, Xenophón Baboúras. 300 m. Medium difficult.

(5) *Kórakas* First ascent up east face, 12 August 1958, by G. Michaelídis, G. Tsamakídis. 200 m. Very difficult.

(6) *Unnamed peak north of Kórakas* First ascent of east edge, 12 August 1958, by Dimitris Liángos, Spýros Antípas, Pétros Semitákis. 200 m. Medium difficult.

(7) *Káto Psiló* First passage of north-west peakline, August 1946, by Yannis and Anna Petróheilos.

(8) *Káto Psiló* First summit ascent and first on east face, August 1939, by Yannis and Ánna Petróheilos, T. Gibbons.

(9) *Gidovoúni* First ascent up west cliff, 14 August 1958, Dimítris Liángos, Alékos Kotsábassis. 300 m. Difficult.

(10) *Pláka Pyramídas* Two new routes up east cliff, by G. Michaelídis and Spýros Antípas; George Tsamakídis and Pétros Semitákis respectively. 350 m. Medium difficult.

119

Peaks from left to right: Skórda, Liontári, Aitós, and 2437.

(11) *Páno Piló* First and only ascent of west face, 22-23 October 1966, by George Michaelídis, Deméstikas. 12 $\frac{1}{2}$ hours with bivouac. Very difficult.

(12) *Kentrikí Soúfla* First ascent of north-west face, summer 1936, by Kaísar Alexópoulos, Kóstas Nátsis, Ánna Petróheilos. Medium difficult.

(13) *Kentrikí Soúfla* First ascent of north cliff, 15 August 1958, by rope climbers George Tsamakídis, Alékos Kotsámbassis. 350 m. Difficult. Also by G. Michaelídis, Dimítris Liángos. 250 m. Medium difficult.

(14) *Kentrikí Soúfla* First ascent of south cliff, in 1936, by Antónis Marínos, Nikos Perrákis. Medium difficult.

(15) *Kentrikí Soúfla* New route on south face, 15 August 1958, by G. Tsamakídis, A. Kotsámbassis. 350 m, 7 hours. Very difficult.

Winter ascents in the Vardoúsia mountains, from December to April, are also very interesting. This season, with the uncertain quality of the snow and sudden changes in weather, provides plenty of challenges.

Winter ascents are usually made from the hostels at Pittimáliko through the Pórtes couloir of Méga Kámbos, and from there to the Kórakas peak. Very few winter climbs have been made on the western group.

Above: Southern group of the Vardoúsia mountains, with Kórakas peak in the centre, as seen from the east. *Below:* Peak Dónti toù Kóraka, as seen when approaching Kóraka peak.

Sunset in the woods of Aghía Marína on the flanks of Mt Imittós. In the distance, a section of Athens and the Bay of Pháliron.

THE MOUNTAINS OF ATTICA

Athens lies in the beautiful plain of Attica which, unfortunately, is in danger of being swallowed up by the inexorable growth of the sprawling Greek capital. The plain is ringed round by mountains, not high but interesting for their many natural beauties and a pleasure to visit.

Mt Imittós (1,026 m)

Better known in English as Mt Hymettus, this is a long mountain stretching to the east of Athens. There is a road all the way to the top now, which offers the chance of a quick excursion by car.

Starting from the suburb of Kaisarianí, it passes through woodland of different conifers, and ten minutes later arrives at the disused but well-kept Kaisarianí monastery.

The monastery buildings as a whole, and the lovely little Byzantine church with excellent frescoes over every inch of its walls and ceilings, are well worth a brief visit. The monastery grounds are richly stocked with big white poplars, planes and other trees, many of them grown to venerable heights and ages. There are flowers everywhere, tended by the Athens Society of the Friends of Trees.

Five minutes beyond Kaisarianí monastery lies the Kallopoúla spring which is famous for its excellent water. Ten minutes further on by car is the Asteríou monastery, another small Byzantine foundation.

Finally the road reaches a saddle from which the far side of the mountain can be seen, and then, turning south, it winds towards the Évzonas summit.

Mt Imittós can, of course, also be climbed on foot, along the same pleasant road. The walk up takes about ninety minutes. Other possible starting points are the bus terminals at Aghía Marína and at Ághios Yánnis Karréas. An enjoyable outing is to walk the length of the mountain along the summit ridge, starting from Ághios Yánnis Kinigós close to the suburb of Aghía Paraskeví, and ending at Aghía Marína, Liópessi (Peanía), or even more southerly at one or other of the shore suburbs.

Another way up is from the east, from the village of Peania (Liópessi). On the slopes of the mountain close to Liópessi is the Koutoúki cave, which is run by the National Tourist Organisation. There is a good dirt road right up to the entrance to the cave.

Mt Imittós has other, though less spectacular caves, and a number of spots suitable for teaching rock climbing. The best-known of these is in the area called Trípios vráhos ("holey rock") in lovely pine woods above the suburb of Aghía Marína.

Mt Pendéli (1,109 m)

Pendéli is a conical mountain which sits on the north-east side of Athens. It is internationally famed for the pure white marble quarried there. All of the Athens Acropolis is built of Pendelian marble, and the same stone was used for many of the famous sculptures of antiquity. But the fame of Pendéli has been its undoing: the mountain is now a sad sight, with all its flanks gouged by the big scars of quarries.

To go up Mt Pendéli, start from the suburb of Paleá Pendéli, from where a dirt road leads almost all the way to the summit.

Another route starts from the north, from the summit resort of Diónyssos, where the houses are built among pines. The part goes through pine woods or scrubland with strawberry trees, honeysuckles etc., and finishes up at the Bíriza spring, a beautifully green place among large shady pines. From here, the is about an hour's walk away.

Mt Párnitha (or Párnes, 1,413 m)

Párnitha is the most beautiful of the Attica mountains, and the pride of Athenian mountain lovers. It is not a high mountain, but its great length gives plenty of scope for extended walks. Párnitha is pleasantly cool even

The mountain hostel on Mt Párnitha below the Órnio peak.

in the height of summer, being almost completely covered by dense forest of Greek fir on the higher reaches, and Aleppo pines further down.

Mt Párnitha has a rich and varied flora. The number of plant species growing on its slopes and peaks is estimated at about a thousand—one-sixth of the total of endemic Greek plant species. The fauna includes a great number of birds, but is poor in mammals. The wolves, roe deer, wild cats and lynxes which formerly lived on the mountain have quite disappeared, with the exception of a few roe deer which are strictly protected by the law.

It should be noted that the greater part of Mt Párnitha is a National Forest, and all grazing, hunting, and tree-cutting is prohibited.

Bubbling mountain stream in the Kleistón gully below the Àrma rocks.

A motor road which starts out from the Athens suburb of Aharnés (or Menídi) zig-zags up to a place called Aghía Triáda, lying at 1,100 m. Here are the beautiful little church of the Holy Trinity which has given the place its name, a tourist kiosk, and the sparkling waters of a spring flowing under enormous beeches and white poplars.

Beyond Aghía Triáda the road forks. The right branch continues to the twin summits known as Karambóla and Órnio, where there are various military stations and a telecommunications tower. A little further up along this road is a turn-off for the hotel and casino Mont Parnés. Another twenty minutes' farther along by car, always through fir woods, is a plateau at 1,150 m with a hostel of the Greek Alpine Club of Athens. The hostel offers food and overnight accommodation to all visitors, together with a fine bird's-eye view over Athens. The summits of Mt Párnitha are further along the same road, overlooking the city on the one side, and the mountains and the sea of Euboea (pron. *Évvia* in Greek) on the other.

Another route that can be taken by car is the circular dirt road which starts out from Aghía Triáda, passes the Paliohóri spring, continues to the Móla tableland on the other side of the mountain with a spring and a church to Ághios Pétros, and eventually comes out on the Aghía Triáda road to the top, which is the return route to Athens.

ROUTES FOR WALKING

Some of the more usual walking routes on Mt Párnitha are as follows.

From the vicinity of Thrakomakedónes on the south side of the mountain there is a good way up through the Hoúni gully, the path being marked with red patches on the trees all the way to the hostel of the Greek Alpine Club of Athens. Walking time is three hours.

Alternatively, begin from the Párnitha road in the Aharnés suburb (Menídi), and turn off it to the west shortly before it starts to climb the mountain. Continue through the attractive Keramídi gully, where after two hours' walking a plateau is reached with poplars and plane trees, a little church to Ághios Yeórgis, and a spring. From here the path turns north to climb uphill, passes through a big stand of pines and comes to a saddle. The rocky peak of Kyrá lies to the right and can be climbed in half an hour. Continuing along the path from the saddle finally leads to Aghía Triáda.

Another pleasant ascent on foot starts from the north side of the mountain, from the Malakássa train station. The well-defined path passes through truly lovely scenery with strawberry trees and other shrubs at first, later with pines, and higher up still with fir trees. After about $4^1/_2$ hours' walking it arrives at the Móla tableland and meets up with the circular dirt road.

A very easy but specially beautiful route goes to the Skípiza spring in the very heart of Mt Párnitha. Setting out from the Greek Alpine Club hostel, go downhill along the Aghía Triáda road a little way, as far as a fork to the right. This leads to a military base and, after going along for about half a kilometer, comes to the turn-off on the right which goes to the Skípiza spring. This is reached in another hour or so. At Skípiza three other paths meet: one from the Paliohóri spring, one from Móla, and one from the circular road via the Platána spring.

The routes given above by no means exhaust all the possibilities of going up Mt Párnitha, which lack of space does not permit to be given here.

ROCK CLIMBING

There are four localities on Mt Párnitha which are particularly suitable for teaching rock climbing.

The northern rock group of Árma, looming over the Kleistón gully.

1. *Árma:* A number of vertical faces above the Kleistón gully, close to the monastery of the same name. They are reached from the village of Hasiá. It is also pleasant to proceed down the gully itself, alternating rappel with dips into the cool water of the stream running along its bottom.

2. *Phlamboúri:* A series of vertical faces east of the gully of Hoúni.

3. *Megalo Arméni:* A peak on the north side of the mountain, close to the village of Kakosálesi.

4. *Pétra Varymbópis:* The formal rock school of the Greek Alpine Club of Athens, this is a group of rocks with varying grades of difficulty, the routes etched into the stone with arrows. Below the rocks is a small hostel where up to ten people can spend the night.

127

THE MOUNTAINS OF THE PELOPONNESE

Mt Zíria (or Kyllíni, 2,376 m)

Mt Zíria is the mountain closest to Corinth and part of a range of mountains which forms a highland barrier in the Northern Peloponnese, running paralled with the shores of the Corinthian gulf. It is made up of two main sections, Mikrí and Megáli Zíria, separated from each other by a deep defile.

The classical ascent to the highest peak, the Simío summit, is made from the Zíria plateau, which can be reached by car from Corinth via Xylókastro and the villages of Réthi, Káto Tríkala, Messéa Tríkala and Áno Tríkala. The journey from Áno Tríkala to the Zíria plateau is thirty minutes by car, or two-and-a-half hours on foot.

On the plateau, which lies at 1,600 m, is a large hostel of the National Federation of Ski and Alpinism and a ski centre of the Greek Tourist Organisation is under construction, to be operational by 1980.

A path from the plateau leads in two-and-a-half to three hours to the summit and passes yet another small hostel. The return is usually made back along the same way.

This route is not, unfortunately, particularly attractive, because the mountain is forested only on its lower slopes. Nothing grows above the plateau, even such grass as there is being cropped completely bare by sheep. It is only in winter that this route is rather splendid, with vast unbroken expanses of snow glistening all around and providing excellent long ski runs.

Other routes for ascending Megáli Zíria can be taken from the villages of Kastaniá south of the mountain, or Goúra west of it.

The route up Mikrí Zíria (2,089 m) starts out from Kephalári village on the east side of the mountain.

The ascents of Mts Mikrí Zíria and Megáli Zíria can be combined by setting out from Kephalári and winding up in Áno Tríkala or on the plateau.

Mt Helmós (or the Aroánia mountains, 2,355 m)

Mt Helmós in Achaëa west of Mt Zíria is properly speaking a mountain group, with many peaks set all around the great ravine of the waters of the Styx, or Mavronéri ("black waters"), which cuts towards the north.

The summit of Psilí Korphí (2,355 m) lies in the most easterly line of peaks, and very close to it, further east still, is the Aïtoráhi peak (2,355 m). North of Psilí Korphí is the mountain known as 2315.

The western peakline includes the second-highest point in the Helmós massif, the Neraïdórahi peak (2,341 m), which is the northern end of the

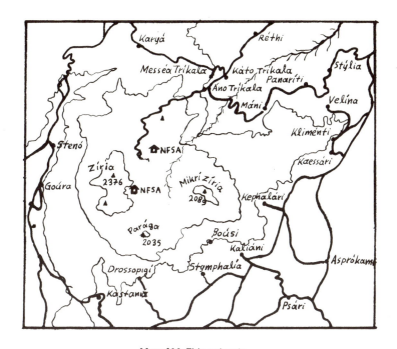

Map of Mt Ziria and environs.

line. The ridge of Neraïdórahi runs southwards and rises again to the 2285 peak.

These two main peaklines—eastern and western—meet at a place called Apáno Lithári, where the valley of the Styx begins. There is a shelter to the south-west of Neraïdórahi, and to the north-west of it lies the great tableland of Xerókambos.

One of the routes for climbing the peaks of the Helmós massif starts out from the town of Kalávrita. This is reached by driving along the coastal road from Corinth and passing through Kiáto, Xylókastro, Dervéni to Diakophtó. From here a left turn runs through a number of small villages to arrive at Kalávrita, which has several hotels for spending the night.

From Kalávrita, the way up Helmós starts with a dirt road to the villages of Áno and Káto Loussí. A branch to the left goes to the Xerókambos tableland, where the road ends. The trip from Kalávrita to Xerókambos is about an hour by car. It should be noted that this branch road is passable by car only in summer.

Alternatively, the climb from Diakophtó to Kalávrita can be made by the ratchet railway through the grandiose ravine of the foaming Vouraikós river, and from Kalávryta to Xerókambos by taxi.

The Styx cataract or Mavronéri on Mt Helmós.

From Xerókambos the "dry meadows" of which provide a good base for a camp, take the south path which after two hours' climbing arrives at a hostel, named after the local spring Tou poulioú i vríssi ("bird's spring"). From here it requires another ninety minutes to reach the Neraïdórahi peak, or three hours to the Psilí Korphí summit.

The most attractive ascent in the Helmós mountains begins from the villages of Peristéra or Sólos, which are reached by car from Akráta on the Corinth-Patrás road. From Peristéra or Sólos there are footpaths through fine woods of Greek fir and black pine which arrive at the Diásello tou kinigoú ("hunter's pass"). Straight ahead are the majestic cliffs bordering the waters of the Styx.

From here the path descends precipitously through scree and mountain torrents that rush down from high above. Finally, when it has

The lower end of the Styx cataract, with the entrance to the cave.

petered out altogether, there is a ravine on the left, from which a 200 m high waterfall is visible straight ahead.

To get close to the waterfall requires crossing the river again and climbing up the steep slope on the right. This comes out exactly at the place where the water cascades down over the rock, which has a small cave which in summer shelters a surprising display of flowers. More freezing cold water issues from the cave itself.

The Styx, of course, was the principal river of the underworld in Greek mythology. Styx was one of the river spirits who were daughters of Oceanus, the river supposed to encircle the earth and the Titan progenitor of the gods. Styx and her children aided Zeus in a quarrel with the Titans, in consequence of which she was greatly honoured, and an oath by Styx was held inviolable by the gods. The river Styx, which was

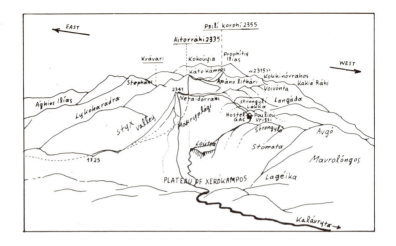

Sketch of the Helmós summits.

thought to be guarded by dragons, came from the realm of the dead and returned there. Its waters were held to possess magical properties.

The continued ascent of the mountains from the waters of the Styx arrives at Apáno Lithári, the juncture of the two main Helmós peak lines where the Styx valley starts. From there óne can go either to the hostel mentioned above, or climb to the left up Psilí Korphí (known in antiquity as Aroánius) or towards the right, up peak Neraïdórahi.

Mt Erýmanthos (2,224 m)

Mt Erýmanthos, west of Mt Helmós, is part of the northern highland barrier in the Peloponnese. It consists of several groups of peaks rather independent of each other, which are widely thought of as separate mountains.

In the western sector of the Erýmanthos range lies the Olenós group—also a name sometimes given to the whole mountain range—the highest peak of which is 2224. South-east of Olenós is the group of peaks known as Psilés Korphés (1,880 m). North-east of the Psilés Korphés is Kalliphóni (1,998 m), and east of Kalliphóni are the Treís gynaíkes ("three women").

To climb Kalliphóny, take the Corinth-Pátras road and turn right at Diakophtó for Kalávrita. From there continue to the village of Káto Vlassía, where the footpath starts. After going through a ravine it arrives ninety minutes later at a spring, and after another half hour at a pass from

On the peaks of Mt Helmós. *Above:* Mountaineering lesson at Neraidórahi peak. *Below:* The alpine zone in June.

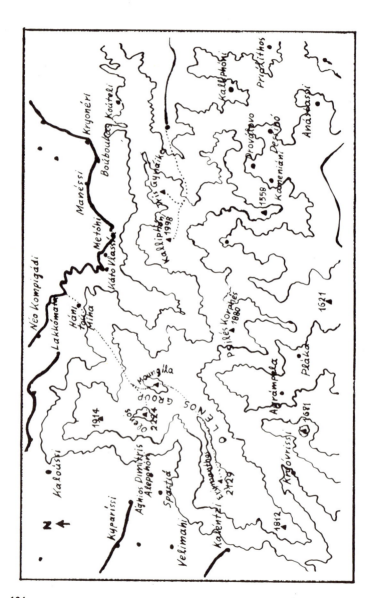

N ←

Kypárissi
Kaloússi
Néo Kompigádi
Lakkómata
Agnos Dimitris Alepphón
Spartiá
Velimáhi
Hámi toú Miha
Káto Vlássa
Metóhi
Maneíssi
Kryonéri
Boúboulas Koútseli
Kallíphon Tris Gyphtariá
▲1998
OLENOS GROUP
Maurigila
Spélaio ▲2224
1914▲
Kaléntzi Erímantha ▲2429
Krýovrissi
1812▲
1691▲
Agrámpela
Psíres Korifés ▲1880
Práka
1621▲
Drováto
Koméniani Der Cibó
▲1558
Kallíphon
Priónlithos
Anastássi

Left: Map of the Erýmanthos mountain group. *Above:* The Ostrakína peak of Mt Ménnalo.

which the peak is clearly visible. It takes another thirty minutes to climb to the top of the cone.

For the peaks of Olenós, take the road from Patrás which climbs through the villages of Halandrítsa, Kállanos, Kallánistra and Lópessi (Katarráhktes), and continue towards Vlassía. Between Lópessi and Vlassía lies the locality of Háni tou Míha, where the climb proper begins, going in a westerly direction.

At first the route passes through the little summer resort of Tsapourniá and then by the Kourembési spring (thirty minutes), and two-and-a-half hours later arrives at a saddle where the highest peak appears on the right. The climb up the final cone to the summit takes about another ninety minutes.

For the Treís gynaíkes group, leave the village of Kértezi (950 m), and take the path through the ravine. One hour's walking arrives at the Ághios Mámmas spring, and another hour at the saddle, which is about thirty minutes away from the peaks.

Mt Ménnalo (1,980 m)

Mt Ménnalo is in fact a quite extensive group of mountains in the central Peloponnese, split into two sections by the Kardará valley. North of this valley is the major bulk of Mt Ménnalo, the highest peak of which is Ostrakína (1,980 m), as well as the Kendrovoúni peak (1,730 m). South of the valley lies the Aintíni group, the top of which is at 1,849 m.

To climb to the summit of the Ménnalo group, start out by taking the Corinth-Argos-Trípoli road, and from Tripoli the road for Levídi as far as a left-hand fork for the almost deserted village of Kardarás. This road, a very well-made dirt track, runs through beautiful woods of Greek fir until it arrives on the Ostrakína plateau, where there is a hostel of the Greek Alpine Club of Tripoli.

From the hostel ascents can be made of the peaks of Ostrakína (thirty minutes) and Kendrovoúni (two hours). In winter, the hostel functions as a flourishing ski centre.

Mt Párnon (1,935 m)

Mt Párnon is a long, narrow mountain with several peaks which drop down in a line parallel to the eastern coast of the Peloponnese. It is a smooth mountain, well forested with Black pine and Greek fir, and with an abundance of wild flowers.

To go up Mt Párnon, take the road from Corinth to Argos to start with, and continue along the coast to Ástros Kinourías. From there a road climbs up the mountain, passing through the village of Ághios Pétros, where accommodation for the night can be found in private houses.

There is also a hostel of the Greek Alpine Club of Spárta halfway along the forest road from Ághios Pétros to Vamvakoú, which can be approached from Spárta via Vamvakoú. To use the hostel, however, permission must have been obtained previously from the Club offices in Spárta.

The walking distance from the shelter to the peak is around two-and-a-half-hours, leading mostly through forest, except for the area just near the top.

The return can be made towards the Malevís convent north of the mountain, which is also a good point of departure for the ascent. The convent is connected with the village of Ághios Pétros by a dirt track.

In the woods of Mt Pangaío.

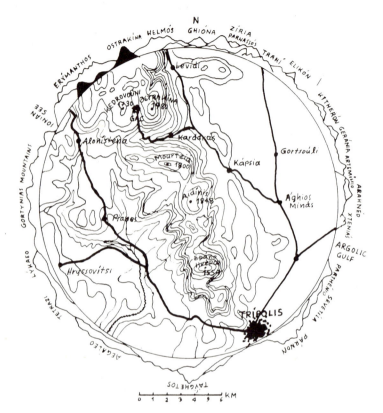

Bird's eye-view map of the peaks of the Mt Ménnalo group, with the Aintínis peak at the centre.

The Taýgetos range (2,407 m)

Taýgetos is the tallest range of the Peloponnese, and its summit one of the longest Greek mountains in terms of mass, being formed of dozens of large peaks in a row. The Taýgetus is divided into a northern and a southern section by the big Langáda ravine, down which runs the Kalamáta-Spárta highway.

In the northern Taýgetos are the peaks Xerovoúna (1,852 m), Xerovoúni (1,521 m), and an unnamed peak (1,612 m) as well as other, lower ones.

It is in the southern Taýgetos, however, that all the great peaks are to be found. Further to the south is the highest of them all, Prophítis Ilías (2,407

The Taýgetos range. *Top left:* Peak Prophítis Ilias. *Top right:* Peak Halasméno vounó. *Bottom:* View of the Taýgetos from the plain of Spárta.

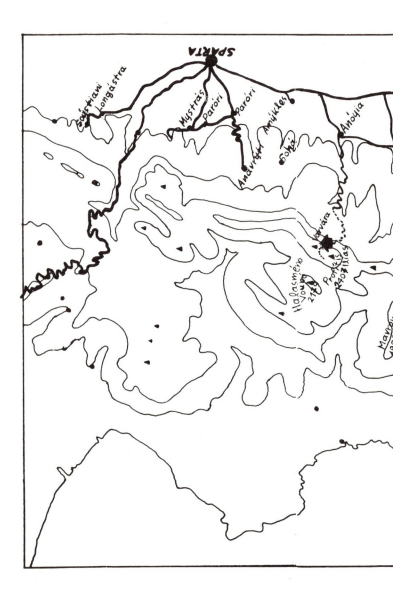

SPARTA

Soustiani
Longástra
Mystrás
Paróri
Paróri
Anávryti Amúkles
Sohá
Anóyia
Haradsméno
Vouni 2148
Proftis 2403Ilías
Varvára
Mavlou

black pines. An overnight stay at the hostel requires previous permission from the Club's offices in Sparta, which will provide the keys.

The ascent of the Prophitis Ilías summit takes two hours from the hostel, and follows a well-defined path.

The Halasméno vounó peak is also well worth visiting. For this, begin from the hostel and follow the same path as for Prophitis Ilías as far as a place called Pórtes. From there, instead of turning right for the peak of Prophitis Ilías, keep going straight north, leaving a gully to your left. About three hours later the route descends down a steep rocky slope to a pass where there are sheep enclosures, and continues by climbing up again to the top of Halasméno vounó from a couloir. The total walking time from Pórtes is five hours or thereabouts.

The descent back to the hostel can also be made towards the highland village of Anavrittí.

Another very interesting excursion is to walk across all the five great peaks of the mountain, which are collectively known as Pendadáktilos ("five fingers"), but this requires spending a night in the open.

THE MOUNTAINS OF MACEDONIA AND THE BORDER REGIONS

Mt Varnoús (or Peristeri, 2,334 m)

This very beautiful mountain straddles the Greek-Yugoslav border, and rises above the lakes known as Mikrí Préspa and Megáli Préspa. The summit of Mt Varnoús is the Kórtsa Toúmba peak (2,334 m).

The slopes and even the peaks of Varnoús are thickly covered with grass in summer, so much so that the mountain looks a deep rich green even from afar.

The ascent of the Kórtsa Toúmba summit begins from Pisodéri village west of Flórina, above the Flórina-Kastoriá road. Two hours' walking from Pisodéri arrives at a pass, and taking the ridge path from there leads to another pass ninety minutes later, from which the peak is clearly visible. Below this second pass there is a spring. From here to the peak it is another hour's climb.

Another peak, the second highest, is Béla Vóda (or in Greek Kaló Neró). This can be climbed in about $2^1/_2$ hours from a place known as Vígla Pisoderíou.

In summer, Mt Varnoús presents no special difficulties. The descent can be made either by the same route, or towards the villages of Krateró and Ethnikó on the east side, which are connected with Flórina by a dirt road which has a bus service.

Mt Kaïmaktsalán (or Vórras, 2,524 m)

The summit of Mt Kaïmaktsalán, one of the highest points in the Greek mountains, forms the boundary between the Greek and the Yugoslav parts of Macedonia. The closest town is Edessa, where one can stay the night. Continuing by car from Edessa towards Flórina goes past the Vegorítida lake and through the small lakeside town of Árnissa, shortly beyond which there is a dirt road on the right leading towards the mountain. It goes as far as the small settlement of Kalívia Yannakoúlia, or just Kalívia, running through a fine forest of enormous trees, known as the Black Forest (Mávro dásos).

At Kalívia begins the ascent on foot, covering bare ground at first as far as the aptly named Sarantóvrissi ("forty springs") plateau at a height of 2,400 m. This plateau has springs bubbling up everywhere. As a result there is plenty of lush grass and every kind of mountain flower all along the way to the peak—a common sight in the Macedónian mountains.

From Sarantóvrissi, the summit of Mt Kaïmaktsalán, the 2524 peak, is reached, lying just inside Yugoslav territory. Exactly at the highest point is a small guesthouse and a little church, which was built from remnants of war materials left after World War I. It was put up in memory of a thousand Yugoslav soldiers who lost their lives in this area in the autumn of 1916 while fighting the Bulgarians, then allies of the Germans. In 1918, the forces of Adad managed to break through the German-Bulgarian front at this point.

Every meter and every centimeter of ground on this peak has been soaked with blood, and even though a great many years have passed since then, it is not unusual to find a spent cartridge or other evidence of those harsh days among the wild violets.

The descent is by the same route.

Mt Vítsi (or Vérno, 2,128 m)

Mt Vítsi rises on the border of the prefectures of Kastoriá and Flórina. The road from Flórina to Kastoriá passes not far from the top of the mountain, north of the village of Perikopí. From there the summit is another ninety minutes away, towards the north of the pass. It is of a regular conical shape, its sides not very steep, and is bare of vegetation— in contrast to the surrounding mountain slopes which are covered in beeches and other trees.

The view from the top is superb. To the east glitters the Vegorítida lake, with the smaller lake of Petrón beside it. To the south-west lies Kastoriá lake, and in the north-west the two great lakes of Mikrí Préspa and Megáli Préspa.

The descent can be made towards Liméria Pávlou Melá to the village of Nymphaío. It is also possible, of course, to use Nymphaío as the starting point for the ascent.

The summit of Mt Voúrinos, seen from the little church of Ághios Pandeleímon.

Mt Syniátsiko (or Áskio, 2,111 m)

To go up Mt Syniátsiko, start by car from Kozáni for Ptolemaída, and from there take the road for the village of Árdasa. The ascent proper begins with a footpath from the village to the unnamed highest point of the mountain, passing through the small hamlet of Bekreveníki. From Árdasa to the peak it is approximately five hours.

Another route is the following: by car from Kozáni to Ptolemaída and to the villages of Anarráhi and Empório. From there, continue as far as the little church at the crossroads before Vlásti village, leave the car, and proceed on foot towards the summit, passing through the locality known as Tsilimíngas.

Mt Voúrinos (1,866 m)

Mt Voúrinos is to the south-west of Kozáni, close to Siátista. Its highest peak is flat-topped like a table, and consists of the brownish-reddish stone known as serpentine. North-east of the summit lies the valley of Messianó Neró, at the bottom of which flows the stream of the same name. On the other side of the valley are the heights of Tsámia and Kakó Prosýlio ("badly exposed to the sun"). The latter has a church to Ághios

145

The two most impressive peaks of Mt Ólympos: Stepháni, or Thróne of Zeus on the left, and the Mýtikas summit peak on the right. Also visible are the Kazánia chasm and the famous rock faces where some very difficult climbs have been made.

Panteleímon, as well as a small guesthouse built by the municipality of Siátista.

To get to the summit of Mt Voúrinos, drive along the Kozáni-Grevená road and stop at the branch-off for Siátista. Here—the place is known as Bára—is also the beginning of a dirt road which, after passing through scrubland badly eroded by goats, reaches a tableland with cultivated fields. This is four hours by car from Bára. The dirt road continues for an hour or so through forested country to the Tsámia spring, very close to the little church of Ághios Panteleímon. Only cars like jeeps can come this far.

An overnight stay can be made camping by the church, or in the neighbouring guesthouse, the keys of which are kept in Siátista where

146

North-east face of the Stepháni peak.

prior arrangements need to have been made. The valley of the Messianó Neró spring and the cone of the summit of Mt Voúrinos are visible from the church.

The valley and the surrounding mountain sides are well-forested with a variety of trees. Only the higher parts of the mountain are bare, but even there a great many wild flowers grow, as they do also in the valley. In fact, the entire valley area is protected, and sheep-grazing, wood-cutting and hunting are not permitted. As a result, the Messianó Neró valley has become a sanctuary for many wild flowers, animals and birds.

To climb to the summit of Mt Voúrinos, take the rough dirt track which starts at the little church by the Tsámia spring and goes right through the valley. A little way down on the right is the path which leads to the top of the mountain. In summer the trek from the spring to the summit takes around three hours.

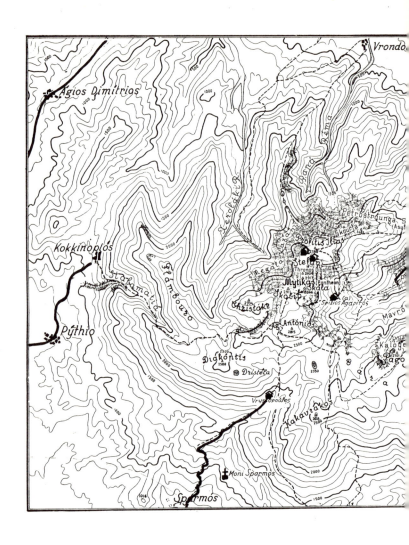

Map of the Ólympos massif.

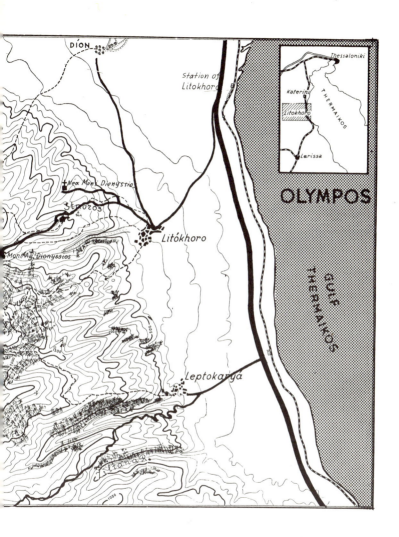

DÍON

Station of
Litokhoro

Néa Moní Dionyssío
Stavros
Moní Ag. Dionyssios

Litókhoro

Leptokaryá

Litohar.

OLYMPOS

GULF
THERMAIKOS

Thessaloniki

THERMAIKOS

Katerini
Litokhoro

Larissa

Ólympos: north edge of peak Stepháni.

The descent can be made either along the same way, with a detour perhaps to visit the Messianó Neró spring in the valley, or north-east down towards the village of Hromió, which involves passing through another valley, bare of major vegetation but with plenty of water.

The Ólympos massif (2,917 m)

Mt Ólympos is the highest Greek mountain, and indeed one of the highest in the whole of the Balkan peninsula. It is not to this, however, that it owes its fame, but rather to the ancient Greeks having believed it to be

150

The cave where the painter Vasílis Ithakísios used to live.

the abode of the gods. They may well have been right—there is no other mountain in Greece with such majestic peaks.

Mýtikas, the very summit of Mt Ólympos, rises to a sharp point over a 450 m deep chasm called Kazánia ("cauldrons"). Around Kazánia, the peaks of Stepháni (2,909 m), Mýtikas (2,917 m), Skála (2,866 m), and Skolió (2,911 m) form a semi-circle. Stepháni— also called Thrónos tou Día ("throne of Zeus")—looks truly like the back of a gigantic armchair against which the god might have leaned to rest. Its western and north-eastern flanks drop down vertically, the former to Kazánia and the latter towards the beautiful plateau of the Muses, where there is also the conical peak of Prophítis Ilías (2,786 m).

Below the great plateau of the Muses lies the wild and gloomy ravine of Mavrólongos, deeply shaded by dark green Balkan pines. This is the source of the Ennippéas (or Ennipévs) river, which winds down the small Kateríni plain to run into the Thermaic gulf.

On the other side of the Mavrólongos ravine, opposite the great peaks, is the Kalóyeros mountain group with the peaks of Págos (2,701 m), and Livadáki (2,366 m). Joining up the two ranges is the Ághios Antónis peak (2,815 m) which closes the ring around the ravine of the Ennippéas river.

Other peaks of Mt Ólympos are Diakóntis (2,588 m) and Kakavrákos (2,618 m) on the Thessalian side of the mountain; Christáki (2,815 m), west of peak Skolió; Toúmba, which is a small projection north of the Stepháni peak; and others of lesser note.

Mt Olympos' nearest neighbours are Káto Ólympos in the south-east, and Mt Piéria in the north-west. To the west it is cut off from Mt Títaros by the Pétra defile. The south-western flanks of Mt Ólympos slope easily to the plain of Elassóna, while north-east of it lies the small Kateríni plain, which has been artificially shored up with soil to stop it eroding away.

The classical summer ascent route to the Mýtikas summit of Mt Ólympos is made from the side of the village of Litókhoro, not far from Kateríni. Litókhoro is reached from the south by taking the Athens-Lárissa highway through the vale of Témby, or from Salonica (Thessaloniki) in the north. From the village of Litókhoro—in a valley of exceptional beauty, where the waters of the river are a reflected viridian green—continue by car for the Dionyssíou monastery, beyond which is a dirt road forking to the left. Following this through the forest leads to a place called Stavrós (at 944 m), where there is a hostel of the Greek Alpine Club of Salonica which is open every day in the summer months.

From Stavrós the road continues through fine woods of black pine to Priónia ("saws"), where there is a small refreshment place and a waterfall. Here the footpath begins which, after passing through splendid mixed woods of black pine and beeches, comes out three hours later at the Spílios Agapitós hostel at 2,100 m. The hostel belongs to the Greek Alpine Club of Litókhoro, and is open all through the summer.

From the Spílios Agapitós hostel it is ninety minutes to the top of Skala peak, and another hour up to the Mýtikas summit. The route from Skala to Mýtikas is rather precipitous, as it is cut into a very steep mountain side. It is nevertheless the easiest way to the summit of Mt Ólympos.

Another route to the top, from the locality Diakládosi, starts about half-way along the Stavrós-Priónia road. The well-defined path from there, which passes through places of inimitable beauty, arrives three hours later at a place called Petróstrounga, and then emerges on bare, open ground at the difficult Skourta pass. About five hours after leaving Diakládosi lies the plateau of the Muses, where there are two hostels: the small and very attractive hostel of the Greek Alpine Club of Kateríni (at 2,650 m), which can be used only after arrangements with the Club offices; and the hostel of the Mountaineering Club of Salonica, which is the largest and at 2,700 m the highest in Greece, open throughout the summer months.

152

Top left: The Kalóyeros group, seen from the Spílios Agapitós hostel. *Top right:* Eastern flank of the Mýtikas peak with the couloir of Mýtikas and Zonária locality. *Bottom left:* The waterfall at Priónia. *Bottom right:* The Kazánia chasm as seen through a gap between Skála and Mýtikas.

The peaks of the Ólympos massif, seen from the Piéria mountain group. *Left to right:* 1. Prophítis Ilias,—2. Toúmba—3. Stepháni—4. Mýtikas—5. Skála—6. Skolió.

From the plateau of the Muses, a path coming down from the Stepháni and Mýtikas peaks meets up with the path from the Spílios Agapitós hostel to the Skála peak. This latter path crosses the so-called Zonária Stephanioú and Zonária Mýtika sites, where the ground is striated horizontally with alternating earth and rocks. Having reached the Stepháni couloir, climb up it to the top of Stepháni, and a little further on, from the Mýtikas couloir, to the Mýtikas summit of Mt Ólympos.

Yet another route, used particularly in winter because it is rather easier, is from the Salonica side of the mountain. Coming by car from Lárissa, take the road for Tírnavo-Elassóna-Kozáni. Shortly after Elassóna there is a right-hand turn to the village of Olympiáda, from where there is another turn which leads to Sparmós village.

154

The Zonária locality, winter and summer.

Beyond Sparmós a dirt track twists up the mountain side to the locality of Vrissopoúles (at 1,900 m), where an army alpine assault unit is quartered, and where there is a hostel belonging to the National Federation of Ski and Alpinism. To stay in this hostel requires permission from the army, or it is possible to set up a tent camp somewhere nearby.

The ascent proper begins along a sloping ridge up to the plateau of Ághios Antónis, above which towers the cone of the peak of the same name, which can either be climbed, or circumvented by going round it to the left through the Ághios Antónis-Christáki pass. Having left the Christáki peak on the right, the Christáki-Skolió pass lies ahead, providing the ascent route to the top of Skolió. Continuing from Skolió along the summit line comes out on the peak of Skála.

The return route is either back along the same way, or towards the Spílios Agapitós hostel, or towards the plateau of the Muses.

Other climbs to the peaks can be made from the villages of Kokkinoplós and Vrontoú. A rather beautiful ascent starts from Litókhoro village and climbs straight up to the peaks of the Kalóyeros group, where there are no hostels.

Mt Ólympos is famous for its rich flora, which includes a great many rare plants, among them several which are endemic specifically to this mountain—such as *Campanula oreadum, Jankea heldreichii,* and *Potentilla deorum.* Once there was also a rich fauna on the mountain, which today has been badly decimated by hunting and poaching. A small herd of chamois *(Rupicapra rupicapra)* and some golden eagles *(Aquilla chryseatos)* have remained, as well as some smaller animals and birds.

A place on Mt Ólympos which should be visited is the old Dionyssíou monastery in the Enníppéa ravine, which was part-ruined by a German bomb in World War II. The monastery is accessible by road. Below the walls of the buildings flow the cool waters of the Enníppéas river, a host of wild flowers on its banks. The surrounding mountain slopes are covered with deciduous woods of every kind of tree, the autumn colouring of which lends a very special beauty to this area.

The largest part of Mt Ólympos—including the highest peaks, the plateau of the Muses, the Mavrólongos area and the Enníppéas ravine—is a protected National Forest, where grazing, tree-felling, hunting, and the cutting of wild flowers is strictly prohibited.

The famous cliffs of the Ólympos peaks provide ascents of considerable difficulty for rock climbers. The main climbs made so far are listed below.

PREVIOUS ASCENTS

(1) *Stepháni* First route up north-east face, 26 June 1934, by E. Comici, A. Escher. Grade 4.

(2) *Stepháni* New route on north-east face, 29 August 1939, by A. Knappe, W. Schwackhofer. Grade 3.

Above: Going up the couloir between the Mýtikas and Stepháni peaks which comes out on the Striv, saddle. *Below:* In the Spílios Agapitós hostel.

(3) *Stephán̄i* New route up north-east face, 18 August 1938, by G. Avanzo, G. Mussafia, G. Trevisini. Grade 4.

(4) *Stephán̄i* New route up north-east face, 6 August 1939, by C. Schwab, N. Agliardi. Grade 3.

(5) *Stephán̄i* New route on north-east face, 11 August 1959, by G. Michaelídis, K. Zolótas, N. Karapatákis. Grade 4.

(6) *Stephán̄i* New route up north-east face, 14 July 1955, by G. Michaelídis, K. Pinátsis. 250 m, 3 hours. Grade 4.

(7) *Stephán̄i* New route up north-east face, 11 August 1961, by G. Michaelídis, T. Baltoúmis, S. Hatziloukás. Grade 4+.

(8) *Stephán̄i* First route upwest face, 21-22 July 1936, by Hans and Sepp Demleitner.

(9) *Stephán̄i* New route up west face, 4 May 1955, by B. Huhn, W.Huhn, H. Wiedmann.

(10) *Stephán̄i* New route on west face, 1-2 August 1956, by G. Michaelídis, G. Xanthópoulos. 400 m, $17^1/_2$ hours. Very difficult.

(11) *Stephán̄i* New route up west face, 3 August 1956, by G. Michaelídis, G. Xanthópoulos. 300 m. $9^1/_2$ hours. Very difficult.

(12) *Stephán̄i* First route on north-west (Comici) edge, 25 June 1934, by E. Comici, A. Escher.

(13) *Stephán̄i* First winter climb of north-west (Comici) edge, 31 December 1959, by D. Liángos, S. Antípas. 250 m, $6^1/_2$ hours. Very difficult.

(14) *Mýtikas* First route up north face, starting from Strivadia pass, September 1930, by K. Nátsis alone.

(15) *Mýtikas* New route up north face, 11 August 1938, by C. Avanzo, G. Mussafia, G. Trevisini.

(16) *Mýtikas* First route up north-west face, 28 June 1934, by E. Comici, A. Escher.

(17) *Mýtikas* New route up north-west face, 3-4 August 1954, by G. Michaelídis, G. Tsamakídis, D. Liángos, P. Idosídis. 450 m, 14 hous. Very difficult.

(18) *Mýtikas* First route up west face, 29-30 July 1957, by G. Michaelídis, K. Zolótas. 450 m, 14 hours. Very difficult.

(19) *Toúmba* First route up west face and on south edge, by G. Michaelídis, G. Xanthópoulos, K. Zolótas. Medium difficult.

(20) *Skolió* First route up north face, 22 July 1934, by M. Lipovsek, Leo Pipan. 6 hours. Fairly difficult.

(21) *Skolió* New route up north face, 19 July 1957, by G. Tsamakídis, D. Liángos, A. Kapetanákis. 500 m, 14 hours. Very difficult.

(22) *Skolió* New route up north face, 16 August 1977, by G. Michaelídis, I. Mavrídis.

(23) *Gólna* First route up north face 29 October 1956, by K. Zolótas, T. Katsamákas, G. Papanikoláou.

West faces of peaks Stepháni and Mýtikas, with all climbings made so far: 1. I. Michaelídis, G. Xanthópoulos—2. H. and S. Demleitner—3. G. Michaelídis, G. Xanthópoulos—4. B. Huhn, H. Wiedmann, W. Huhn.—5. F. Kolar, M. Doubner—6. G. Michaelídis, K. Zolótas—7. A. Spanoúdis, D. Boudólas, P. Tirninís.

(24) *Couloir between Mýtikas and Stepháni from Kazánia,*   First route, August 1933, by G. Soútsos, A. Marínos, D. Haniótis.

Mt Piéria (2,190 m)

This is a very attractive mountain north-north-west of Ólympos, densely forested mainly with beeches but also with other species of tree. Its major peaks lie in a straight line running north to south. The highest is peak Phlámbouro (2,190 m) in the southern reach. Mt Títaros (1,839 m) may be considered a continuation of Piéria, lying between it and Mt Ólympos.

The ascent of the Piéria summit starts from Kateríni along the Elassóna road. Some way along there is a right-hand fork for the village of Messaía Miliá. Continue from the village along a forest dirt track as far as Epáno Miliá, a village of which only the church now remains. A little higher up

North-east face of peak Stepháni, with all climbings made up to now. 1. E. Comici, A. Escher—2. R. Knappe, W. Schwackhofer—3. G. Michaelidis, A. Eggler, E. Eggler, K. Michaelídou—4. G. Schwab, N. Agliardi—5. G. Michaelídis, K. Pinátsis—6. G. Michaelídis, K. Zolótas, N. Karapatákis—7. G. Michaelídis, T. Baltoúmis, S. Hatziloukás.

lies the hostel of the Greek Alpine Club of Kateríni, one of the largest and best hostels in Greece today, which after previous arrangements with the Club's offices provides accommodation for the night.

From the hostel the forest road continues for a few kilometers up to where the path for the summit starts out, which is clearly marked and easily followed. It first goes in a north-westerly direction, and then veers west until it arrives on the mountain ridge, where it turns south. Following the ridge leads to the Phlámbouro summit. The main part of the route is through forest, with only the last part on bare ground. From the hostel to the top of Phlámbouro peak requires roughly three to four hours.

The return is by the same route.

A fine ascent can also be made from the side of the prefecture of Kozáni, starting out from the village of Kataphígio.

Mt Phalakró of Dráma (2,232 m)

There is no doubt that Mt Phalakró, close to Dráma town, is among the most beautiful of the Macedonian mountains. Its lower slopes are green with forests, while higher up it is bare. However, "bare" is hardly the right word, since all the slopes right up to the very top of the peaks are carpeted with soft grass, which myriad of wild flowers everywhere turn into a vast alpine garden.

The Greek veteran mountain climber, G. Michaelídis, on the north face of the Skolió peak, with the Mýtikas summit beyond. (Photo G. Mavrídis)

Mt Piéria. *Above:* The Áno Miliá hostel. *Below:* Winter woods.

Mt Piéria is mostly covered with woods of black pine, Macedonian fir and beech.

The highest peaks of the Phalakró mountain group form a semi-circle around a chasm which somewhat resembles that of Kazánia on Mt Ólympos. The summit peak is known as 2232. To the west of it lies the Hionótripa (2111 m), and further west still is Kartálka, little more than 2,000 m high. Between 2232 and Kartálka is a flat crater several meters each in depth and diameter, which continues to hold snow until August. It is suitably called Hionótripa ("snow hole").

The climb to the summit of Mt Phalakró starts out by car to Dráma, and from there to the village of Vólakas. From Vólakas the route continues on foot, passing at first through fields until it comes to forest and, still in a south-easterly direction, finally comes out on the bare saddle of Kourí

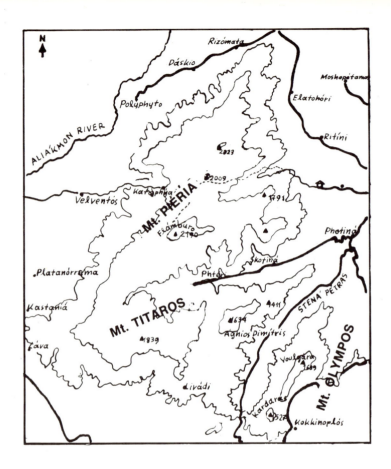

Map of Mt Piéria, Mt Títaros and environs.

(1,400 m), east of the peak of the same name (1,456 m). Here there is a small, half-finished hostel.

The path from the saddle now veers to the north-east and crosses a small wood to begin with, until it emerges on meadow land, going gently uphill as far as the small hostel at the Horós locality (at 1,700 m), where up to eighteen people can spend the night after prior arrangements with the Greek Alpine Club of Dráma.

From the hostel, the path continues to the plateau of Ághio Pnévma ("Holy Ghost") where herds of cows are put to graze, and then runs in an

Above: Sheep dog on Mt Piéria. *Below:*Cattle drinking on the Ághio Pnévma plateau of Mt Phalakró.

The flower meadows on Mt Phalakró.

easterly direction to the north of the peaks Hionótripa and 2232. Close to 2232 turn right, and climb up the southern rise. From here a fantastic view is spread out below.

The area may justly be termed a botanical paradise, and contains rare plants such as *Gentiana verna* (spring gentian), *Viola delphinantha, Haberlea rhodopensis, Campanula orphanidea, Achillea ageratifolia, Dryas octopetala* (mountain avens), and *Daphne rosaninii* and others.

Lately a road has been built straight to the Ághio Pnévma plateau , where a ski centre is being set up.

There is another hostel on the northern side of the mountain, at Bartíseva (1,142 m), which is reached by forest road from the village of Vólakas. It has sixteen beds, and also belongs to the Greek Alpine Club of Dráma.

166

Looking south from the 2232 peak of Mt Phalakró.

Mt Pangaío (1,956 m)

This is another of the attractively wooded mountains of Macedonia. A forest road goes right up to the summit known as Piláf Tepé (1,956 m), where there is a television relay station. This road starts from the Akrovoúni village, which lies above the Salonica-Kavála road.

Other high points on Mt Pangaío are Rhodolívos (1,927 m), Máti (1,836 m), Koumbilí (1,724 m), and an unnamed peak of 1,910 m. Rhodolívos and Koumbilí both have good cliffs for rock climbing.

A very pleasant ascent can be made from the village of Avlí, which is again on the Salonica-Kavála road. The path from Avlí goes through forests of beeches and glades full of giant ferns as high as a man. It takes

The Rhodolívos peak of Mt Pangaío.

$3^1/_2$ hours' walking to the Argýris Petaloúdas hostel (at 1,550 m), just off the motor-road to the top. There is room for twenty-five people to spend the night, after arrangements have been made with the Greek Alpine Club of Kavala. From the hostel to the peak it is another hour or so on foot.

Another good route to the summit sets out from the village of Nikísiani. The path follows along the right side of a stream as far as the locality of Livádia (at 465 m), where there is a spring. Then it crosses the stream, climbs up on the left, and comes out at a pass (1,620 m) between the peaks of Piláf Tepé and Máti, from where the top of either can be reached.

Mt Órvilos (2,212 m)

Órvilos straddles the Greek-Bulgarian border, and its highest peak forms the boundary between the prefectures of Sérres and Dráma.

In the splendid woods of Mt Párnon.

Mt Pangaío is renowned for its rich vegetation and the beauty of its many wild flowers. One of these is *Lilium martagon,* which grows up to 1.5 m tall.

To climb to the top, start from Dráma by car and drive north to the village Káto Nevrokópi. From there a dirt track goes westward to the villages of Vathítopos and Katáphito. From Katáphito a roughly three-hour climb in a north-westerly direction leads to the summit peak of Alí Boutoús, which is bare of trees.

The slopes of Mt Órvilos are thickly covered with different species of fir and mountain pine. Where there are no trees, lush green meadows are rich in every kind of wild flower, so that it is difficult to know where to tread.

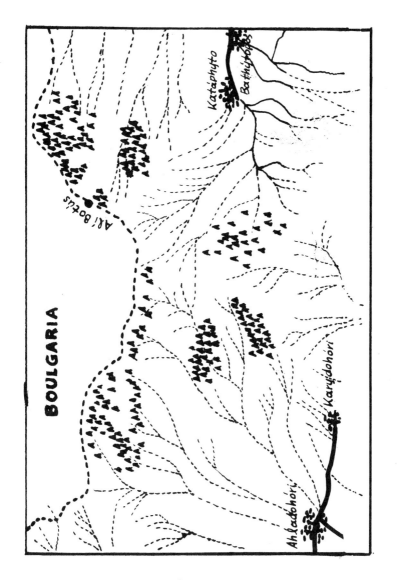

Sketch-map of Mt Órvilos with peak Alí Boutoús.

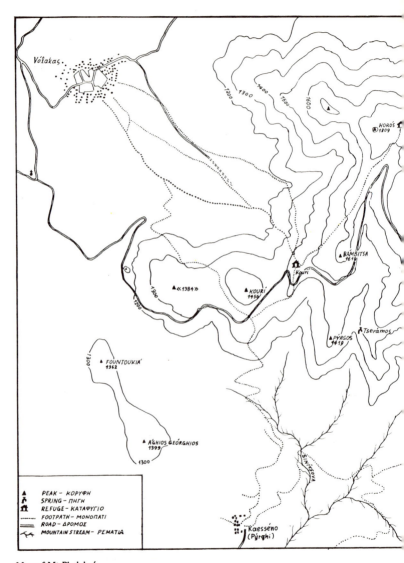

Map of Mt Phalakró

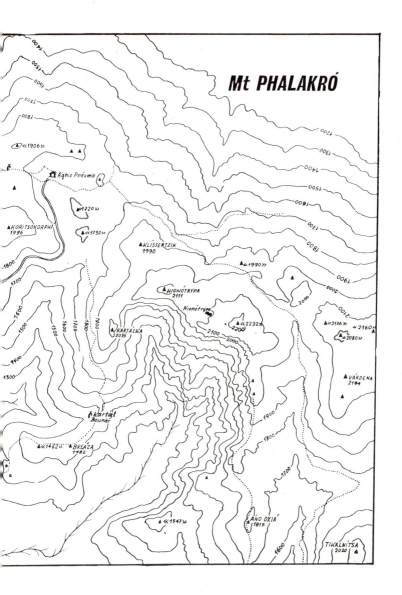

Mt PHALAKRÓ

«1906»

Aghio Pnévma

«1720»

▲ KORITSOKORPHÍ
1996

«1730»

▲ KLISSENTZIK
1990

«1990»

▲ HIONÓTRYPA
2111

Hionótrypa

«2232»
2200

«2176»   «2160»
2080»

▲ KARTALKA
2035

2100
2000

▲ VARDENA
2194

Kartál
Bounar

«1462»   ▲ BREAZA
1482

«1547»

ÁNO OXIA
1817

TIKALNITSA
2020 ▲

THE MOUNTAINS OF CRETE

The White Mountains (or Madáres, 2,453 m)

The summit of the Lefká Óri ("white mountains")—also known as Madáres—is the second-highest point in Crete, only three meters lower than Mt Psilorítis (or Idi, and in English generally known as Mt Ida). Though Psilorítis takes precedence in terms of height, the Whiter Mountains are very much more interesting. They lie on the west side of the island in the prefecture of Haniá, and include dozens of major peaks.

The summit peak is Páchnes (2,453 m). North-east of this lies the Troháris peak (2,401 m), and in the south-west the peak of Zaranokephála (2,140 m). North-east of the Páchnes summit is an unnamed height, and beyond that the peak of Griás Sorós (2,331 m). Further east is yet another nameless mountain, followed along roughly the same line by peak Kástro (2,218 m). North of Páchnes and north-west of Griás Sorós lies the Mávri peak (2,065 m).

All of the above are in the group of the White Mountains which might be designated the eastern range. A second group is to the north-west of this, seperated from the first by a north-to-south ravine which ends in the great gorge of Samariá. This second group includes the peaks of Melindaoú (2,133 m), Kallóros (1,925 m), and two nameless mountains, and may be called the central range.

A third group of mountains is to the west of the Páchnes summit peak, and is cut off from the other two by the gorge of Samariá. This may either be described as the western range, or considered as the independent mountain massif Volakiás with the highest peak Volakiás (2,116 m). North-west of peak Volakiás lie the peak Gíngilos (2,080 m), and further west is Psiláphi (1,983 m).

Gíngilos easily offers the greatest interest for rock climbers, and many expeditions have been made there by Greek and foreign mountaineers.

To go to the White Mountains, take the road from Haniá via the villages of Aghía Fournés, Lákkos etc. and as far as Omalós village at the edge of a plateau of the same name. From here a dirt road crosses the plateau to the locality of Xylóskalo, where there is a tourist kiosk. About half-way along this fifteen-minute car drive from Omalós is a fork on the left, which leads to the Kallérgi hostel. Use of the hostel requires previous arrangements with the Greek Alpine Club of Haniá. There is also a footpath which leads straight to the hostel from Omalós.

This hostel is the starting point for ascents of the eastern and central range of the White Mountains.

The Lefká Óri, to give them their Greek name, are dry and bare and have very few springs, so it is necessary to go well provided with drinking water. The best season for climbing them is from mid-April, when there is still quite a lot of snow, until the middle of June, after which it gets very hot. There are a good number of rare wild flowers on the top of the mountains, often endemic to that particular peak, or at least endemic to Crete.

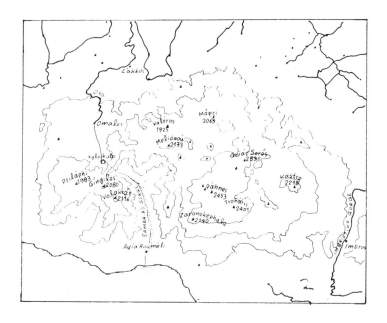

Map of the White Mountains and the gorge of Samariá.

The Gorge of Samariá

To reach the gorge of Samariá, go by car up to the Omalós plateau and continue to the Xylóskalo tourist kiosk. Here overnight camp can be made. From Xylóskalo a very well-defined path drops down into the gorge.

About ten minutes after setting out there is a spring, and after another thirty minutes a second spring, known as Ríza Sikiás ("figtree root"). About ninety minutes from Xylóskalo lies the little church of Ághios Nikólaos. From here the path continues along the bottom of the gorge to the now deserted village of Samariá. Farther along lies the narrowest point, called Pórtes, beyond which the gorge broadens again until the village of Aghía Roúmeli is reached. The route takes about three hours walking in all.

The gorge, one of the finest in all of Europe, is richly wooded with cypress and pine trees. It is also the habitat of the Cretan wild goat *(Capra aegagnus cretensis)* which is unique in the world, and for the sake of which the area has been declared a protected National Forest.

175

Peak Gíngilos and the gorge of Samariá. (Photo Michael Christodoúlou)

Hostel at the Vólikas locality in the White Mountains. (Photo George Moisidis)

Mt Psilorítis (or Ídi, 2,456 m)

Mt Psilorítis (in English generally Mt Ida) is the highest of the Cretan mountains, topping the summit of the White Mountains by just three meters. There is a popular story that Haniá mountaineers, wishing to correct this discrepancy in their favour, began to carry stones up the White Mountains to raise the Páchnes summit peak above that of Mt Psilorítis. If they have succeded, international recognition of their feat is still outstanding.

In contrast to the much broken-up peak line of the White Mountains, Mt Psilorítis appears as a continuous long and narrow highland mass.

To get to the summit peak of Mt Ídi, go by car from Réthymno or from Iráklion (Heraklion) along the road joining these two towns, as far as the turn-off for the large village of Anógia. From there, continue along a dirt road to the place known as Nída (a derivation of the ancient word Ídi), where the Idian cave is where the goat Amaltheia is said to have suckled the infant Zeus (see chapter on mythology).

From Nída a path to the south, which later veers west, leads gradually to the summit in something like five hours.

177

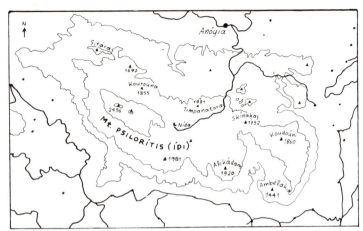

Map of Mt Psiloritis.

Cretan wild goat (*Capra aegagrus cretensis*), which lives in the gorge of Samaria.

Map of Mt Díkti (or the Lasithiótika mountains).

Mt Díkti (or Lasithiótika Vouná 2,148 m)

Mt Díkti lies at the border of the prefectures of Iráklion and Lasíthi, with its highest point in the territory of the latter.

To climb to the summit, approach by car from Iraklion or from Neápoli, and take the turn-off through the villages of Mohós, Krási, Kéra and Lagoú to Tzermiádo village. Continue through the tiny hamlets of Lasíthi and Lasitháki, as far as the village of Ághios Geórgios, from which there is a footpath for the summit, setting off in a southerly direction.

This path arrives ninety minutes later at the locality of Limnákaro, and then continues south. Approaching the peak, turn left towards the south-east. From the beginning of the footpath at Ághios Geórgios to the summit peak (2, 148 m) of Spathí ("sword") or Parathíri ("window") requires approximately four hours. Very close to the top of the mountain on the east side is an unnamed peak, and to the south-west the peak of Afféndis Christós (2,141 m).

The author during the ascent of Mt Gamíla.

Part III

REFERENCE SECTION

INDEX OF GREEK MOUNTAINS

Readers are requested to employ some ingenuity with respect to the transliterated names, as there are no hard and fast rules for rendering Greek sounds in Latin letters. Generally speaking, the spelling here used reproduces the spoken sound—i.e. μπ = B, β = V, χ = H, αι = E or Ai, and φ = Ph. The word óri, where it has been retained, means mountains. Very well-known place names are given in English. The prefecture or area referred to in the following index is the one where the highest peak of the mountain is found.

CRETE

name of mountain	height in m	prefecture or area
Agathés	1,511	Haniá
Apopygádi	1,311	Haniá
Dikti or Lasithiótika Vouná	2,148	Lasithi
Kédros	1,777	Réthymno
Kouloúkonas	1,083	Réthymno
Koutroúlis	1,071	Haniá
Kóphinas	1,231	Iráklion
Krioneritis	1,312	Réthymno
Lefká Óri (see White Mountains)		
Ornó	1,237	Lasithi
Psyloritis (or Idi)	2,456	Réthymno
Selléna	1,559	Lasithi
Sidérotas	1,136	Réthymno
Thrýptis Mountains	1,476	Lasithi
Volakiás	2,116	Haniá
White Mountains	2,453	Haniá

EUBOEA (EVVIA)

Aloktéri	1,096	Central Euboea
Dirphi	1,743	Central Euboea
Kandili	1,246	Central Euboea
Mavrovoúni	1,189	Central Euboea
Óhi	1,398	Southern Euboea
Ólympos	1,172	Central Euboea
Pixariás	1,343	Central Euboea
Skotini	1,362	Central Euboea

Mt Xerovoúni in Central Euboea, seen from the Dírphi hostel.

Teléthrio	970	Northern Euboea
Xerovoúni	1,417	Central Euboea
Xyró	991	Central Euboea

AEGEAN AND IONIAN ISLANDS

Ainos	1,628	Kephalloniá
Atávyros	1,215	Rhodes
Ipsári	1,203	Thássos
Karvoúnis	1,153	Sámos
Kérkis (or Kerketévs)	1,433	Sámos
Kouvára (or Pétallo)	1,003	Ándros
Lástos	1,215	Kárpathos
Mélissa	1,033	Ikaria
Pellinéo *	1,297	Chios
Phengári (or Sáos) * *	1,600	Samothráce
Stavrotá * * *	1,158	Lefkáda
Vounó (or Drios)	1,008	Náxos

* Height not absolutely certain, and for lack of information taken from commercial maps.
* * One school of thought gives Sáos as the name of the mountain, with Phengári that of the summit peak.
* * * Height also sometimes given as 1,141 m.

THE PELOPONNESE

Agriokerasiá	1,143	Arcady
Aphrodissio	1,147	Achaïa
Arachnaio	1,199	Argolis
Artemissio	1,771	Argolis
Bakhriámi	1,031	Argolis
Dourdouvána	2,109	Achaïa-Corinthia
Ellinitsa	1,297	Arcady
Erýmanthos	2,224	Achaïa
Helmós (or Aroánia óri)	2,341	Achaïa
Hteniás	1,634	Arcady-Argolis
Kaláthio	1,490	Messinia
Kalliphóny *	1,998	Achaïa
Kerasiá	1,098	Arcady
Klokós	1,779	Achaïa
Koulohéra * *	1,125	Lakonia
Lámbia	1,797	Ilia
Lýkaio	1,428	Messinia-Arcady
Lyrkio	1,648	Arcady-Argolis
Madára * * *	1,297	Lakonia
Marmáti	1,780	Achaïa
Mavronóros	1,757	Corinthia
Megalovoúni	1,273	Argolis-Corinthia
Ménnalo	1,980	Arcady
Minthi	1,345	Ilia
Oliyirtos	1,935	Arcady-Corinthia
Óri Kyparissias	1,151	Messinia
Ortholithi	1,105	Argolis
Panahaïkó	1,926	Achaïa
Párnon (or Malevós)	1,935	Lakonia-Arcady
Pharmakás	1,616	Argolis
Psili Ráhi	1,068	Corinthia
Rezénikos	1,274	Arcady
Saitás	1,814	Arcady-Achaïa
Skiadovoúni	1,428	Ilia-Achaïa
Ziria (or Ķyllini)	2,376	Corinthia

* Kalliphóny may be considered a branch of Erymanthos.
* * Mountain at the most southerly end of the Párnon range.
* * * This mountain is a continuation of the Parnon range, which from it is separated, by the Mari valley.

CENTRAL GREECE

Eastern Ágrapha *	2.042	Evritania
Kithairónas	1,409	Megaris-Viotia
Klókova	1,039	Aitoloakarnania

Knimída (or Spartiás)	938	Phthiotis
Korobíli	908	Viotia
Lykomnímata	1,522	Evritania- Phthiotis
Mártsa	1,690	Evritania- Phthiotis
Messápio	1,021	Viotia
Nartháḵi	1,011	Phthiotis -Thessaly
Oïti	2,152	Phthiotis -Thessaly
Óri Lidorokioú	1,911	Phokis
Óri Nafpaktias	1,472	Aitoloakarnania
Órthrys	1,726	Phthiótis-Thessaly
Oxiá * *	1,926	Aitoloakarnania-Evritania
Palliovoúna (or Pintiza) * * *	1,032	Megaris
Panetolikó	1,924	Aitoloakarnania
Parnassós	2,457	Phthiótis
Párnes (or Párnitha)	1,413	Attica
Pástra	1.016	Attica
Patéras	1,131	Attica
Pendéli	1,107	Attica
Phtéri of Ágrapha	2,128	Evritania
Trikorpho	1,545	Phokis
Tsakaláki	1,712	Aitoloakarnania
Tsekoúra	1,734	Aitoloakarnania
Varássova	915	Aitoloakarnania
Vardoúsia	2,495	Phokis
Veloúhi (or Tymphristós)	2,316	Evritania
Vlahovoúni	1,672	Phokis
Voulgára	1,654	Evritania-Thessaly
Voutsikáki or Agrapha	2,154	Evritania-Thessaly
Yeránia	1,351	Megaris
Yerolékkas	1,714	Phokis
Zagarás (or Motsára)	1,526	Viotia

* Highest peak of the Eastern Ágrapha, names and heights of which are very confused.
* * The correct name is Oxiá and not the mountaineers' Gramméni Oxiá.
* * * Properly a part of the Yeránia mountains.

EPIRUS

Doúsko *	2,198	Ioánnina-Albania
Driskos	1,078	Ioánnina
Gamila (or Týmphi)	2.497	Ioánnina
Grámmos	2,597	Ioánnina-Macedonia -Albania
Kakarditsa	2,469	Ioánnina-Thessaly
Kassidiáris	1,329	Ioánnina
Kléphtes	1,890	Ioánnina
Kléphtis	1,846	Ioánnina

Winter aspect of Mt Elikónas in Central Greece, with the Gulf of Corinth in the distance.

Kokkinólakkos	1,750	Árta
Koukouroútsos	1,785	Ioánnina
Koústa	1,731	Ioánnina
Koutsókrana	1,324	Ioánnina
Lákmos - see Peristéri of Métsovon		
Ligkos or East Pindus * *	2,177	Ioánnina-Macedonia
Makrikambos	1,672	Ioánnina-Albania
Megáli Tsoúka	1,173	Ioánnina
Mitsikélli	1,810	Ioánnina
Óri Kouréndon	1,172	Ioánnina
Óri Paramythiás	1,658	Thesprotia
Óri Souliou	1,615	Thesprotia-Ioánnina
Óri Tsamandá	1,806	Thesprotia-Albania
Óri Váltou	1,852	Árta
Peristéri of Métsovon * * * or Lakmos	2,295	Ioánnina-Thessaly
Pharmakovoúni	1,240	Thesprotia
Prixa	2,048	Ioánnina
Pýrgos Tsougri	1,104	Árta
Smólikas	2,637	Ioánnina
Stoúros	1,559	Ioánnina

Thesprotiká óri	1,274	Préveza
Tómaros (or Olitsika)	1,816	Ioánnina
Trapezitsa	2,022	Ioánnina
Tsoúka Róssa * * * *	1,987	Ioánnina
Tsoumérka	2,393	Árta
Vasilitsa	2,249	Ioánnina-Macedonia
Vounó Malounioú * * * * *	1,020	Thesprotia
V. Mousakaiïkon * * * * *	1,082	Préveza
Vounó Haravgis * * * * *	1,202	Thesprotia
Xerovoúni	1,614	Ioánnina
Zarkorráhi	1,332	Préveza-Ioánnina

* Part of Mt Nemértska in Albania, a section of which is called Mourgána.
* * Five peaks, almost independent mountains, to the north of Métsovo. Normally cartographed separately and rarely listed under the common name of Ligkos. (For names, see note to Macedonia below).
* * * "Lákmos" in high Greek, but known as Peristéri in the surrounding villages. Not to be confused with the Peristéri of Macedonia.
* * * * An independent mountain east of Mt Gamila, unrelated to the Gamila peak of the same name, and usually described on maps as Tsoúka Arósia–an unsuccessful attempt to hellenise the Vlach name of "Red peak".
* * * * * Unnamed on map.

THESSALY

Antihásia	1,424	Trikala
Avgó of South Pindus *	2,148	Trikala
Delidimi of Ágrapha	2,163	Karditsa-Central Greece
Hatzi	2,038	Trikala
Itamos	1,490	Karditsa
Karáva of Ágrapha	2,184	Karditsa
Karavoúla of Ágrapha	1,862	Karditsa-Trikala
Kassidiáris (or Narthákio)	1,011	Lárissa-Central Greece
Káto Ólympos	1,587	Lárissa
Kazárma of Ágrapha	1,971	Karditsa
Kédros	1,796	Trikala
Kissavos (or Óssa)	1,958	Lárissa
Kóziakas	1,901	Trikala
Krátsovo	1,554	Trikala
Mavrovoúni	1,054	Lárissa
Ólympos	2,917	Lárissa-Macedonia
Pilion	1,651	Magnisia
Prophitis Ilias	1,049	Lárissa
Titaros	1,839	Lárissa-Macedonia
Tringia * *	2,204	Trikala
Veroússia	1,835	Karditsa

Top of Mt Dirphis in Euboea.

Voutsikáki of Agrapha   2,154   Karditsa-Central Greece

* The peaks of the mountain (Avgó, Loupata, Marossa) are sometimes
listed as seperate mountains, but in fact form one massif.
* * A large group in the Southern Pindus, with the mountains Tringia,
Neraïda and Mikri Neraïda.

MACEDONIA

Áthos	2,033	Halkidiki
Bélles (or Kerkini)	2,031	Sérres-Bulgaria
Boútsi-Órlovo *	1,776	Flórina
Ditiki ("western") Rhodópi	1,966	Dráma
Dovrás	1,378	Kozáni
Grámmos	2,520	Kastoriá-Épirus-Albania
Hortiátis	1,201	Salónica
Holomóndas	1,165	Halkidiki
Kaïmaktsalán (or Vóras)	2,524	Pélla-Flórina-Yugoslavia
Kamvoúnia	1,615	Kozáni-Grevená
Karangióz	1,055	Dráma
Kotzá	1,115	Dráma
Koúla of Rhodópi	1,827	Dráma-Thrace-Bulgaria
Kroúsia óri (or Dissoro)	1,179	Kilkis-Sérres

Ligkos (Eastern Pindus) * *	2,177	Grevená
Mavrovoúni	1,179	Kilkis-Sérres
Menikio (or Boz Dag)	1,963	Sérres
Moriki	1,703	Kastoriá
Ólympos	2,917	Piéria-Thessaly
Óri Vrontoús (incl. Laï Lia)	1,849	Sérres
Óri Lekánis (or Tsal Dag)	1,298	Dráma-Kavála
Órvilos	2,212	Dráma-Sérres-Bulgaria
Páïko	1,599	Pélla-Kilkis
Pangaio	1,956	Kavála-Dráma
Phalakró (or Boz Dag)	2,232	Dráma
Piéria	2,189	Piéria-Kozáni
Siniátsiko (or Áskio)	2,111	Kozáni
Triklári	1,749	Flórina
Tsingélli (or Ángistro)	1,294	Sérres
Tsouka Karali,	1,231	Grevená
Varnous * * *	2,334	Flórina-Yugoslavia
Vassilitsa	2,249	Grevená-Épirus
Vérmio	2,052	Pélla
Vertiskos	1,078	Salonica
Vitsi (or Vérno)	2,128	Flórina-Kastoriá
Vóïo	1,802	Kastoriá-Kozáni
Voúrinos	1,866	Kozani-Grevená

* Two mountains connected by a pass. The slightly higher Boútsi is in the Florina prefecture, Órlovo is in Kastoriá.
* * The individual peaks (Aftiá, Avgó, Phlénga, Mavrovoúni, Miliá and Pyrostiá) are usually listed separately. It is correct to refer to them as Mt Ligkos, however.
* * * The highest peak of Greece.

THRACE

Anatoliki ("east") Rhodópi *	1,267	Rhodópi-Bulgaria
Achlát Tsal * *	1,490	Xánthi
Koúla of Rhodópi * * *	1,897	Xánthi-Macedonia-Bulgaria
Papiki of Rhodópi	1,484	Rhodópi-Bulgaria
Silo-Sápka * * * *	1,065	Évros-Komotini

* Height given is for peak Megálo Livádi.
* * Including Kyr er Krané, 1,286 m, which can be considered a separate group.
* * * Includes Mt Haïntoú.
* * * * Two mountains linked by a pass.

THE PINDUS RANGE FROM NORTH TO SOUTH

Northern Pindus:

Moráva	—	Albania
Triklári	1,749	Flórina
Grámmos	2,520	Ioánnina-Kastoriá-Albania
Vóïo	1,802	Kastoriá
Kléphtis	1,846	Ioánnina
Smólikas	2,637	Ioánnina
Trapezitsa	2,022	Ioánnina
Vassilitsa	2,249	Ioánnina-Kozáni
Gamila (or Týmphi)	2,497	Ioánnina
Kléphtes	1,890	Ioánnina
Koukouroútzos	1,785	Ioánnina
Ligkos (or East Pindus)	2,177	Ioánnina-Kozáni
Tsoúka Karali	1,231	Grevená
Mitsikélli	1,810	Ioánnina

Southern Pindus:

Peristéri of Métsovon	2,295	Ioannina-Trikala
Kédros	1,796	Trikala
Tringia	2,204	Trikala
Kakarditsa	2,469	Ioánnina-Trikala
Kóziakas	1,901	Trikala
Avgó	2,148	Trikala
Tsoumérka	2,393	Árta
Hatzi	2,038	Trikala
Veroússia	1,775	Karditsa
Karavoúla (Ágrapha)	1,862	Trikala-Karditsa
Kokkinólakkos (Ágrapha)	1,750	Árta
Karáva (Ágrapha)	2,184	Karditsa
Kazárma (Ágrapha)	1,971	Karditsa
Voutsikáki (Ágrapha)	2,154	Karditsa-Evritania
Delidimi (Ágrapha)	2,163	Karditsa-Evritania
Ítamos (Ágrapha)	1,490	Karditsa
Phtéri (Ágrapha)	2,128	Evritania
East Ágrapha	2,042	Evritania
Mártsa (Ágrapha)	1,690	Evritania
Voulgára (Ágrapha)	1,654	Evritania-Karditsa
Lykommimata (Ágrapha)	1,522	Evritania-Phthiótis

MARKED MOUNTAIN PATHS

The markings are dabs of paint on tree trunks, rocks etc., usually in red. One of the most serious problems for the mountaineer in Greece is the absence of good maps. Not surprisingly, a good many people get lost in the mountains, and suffer considerable hardship as a result. To ameliorate this situation, a number of mountain routes have now been marked, and a complete list follows of all ascents known to be marked at the time of going to print.

The Peloponnese:

on Mt Artemission	— from Kariés village to the top
on Mt Dourdouvána	— from Kalivia Pheneoú village to the top
on Mt Helidoréa	— from Ambélia locality to the top
on Mt Klokós	— from Phtéri village to the top
on Mt Oliyirtos	— from Láfka village to the top
on Mt Párnon	— from the Malevis monastery to the top
	— from Ághios Pétros village to the hostel
	— from Vamvakoú village to the hostel
	— from the hostel to the Krónio peak
on Mt Pharmakás	— from the saddle to the top and on to the spring
on Mt Saitás	— from the Máti locality to the top
on Mt Taïgetos	— from Poliánna village to the Varvára hostel and to the Prophitis Ilias peak
on Mt Trahi	— from Alléa village to the top

Central Greece:

on Mt Elikónas	— from Koúkoura village to the top
on Mt Ghióna	— from Kaloskopi village to the top
on Mt Helidóna	— from the river before the old village of Mikró Horió to the top.
on Mt Kallidromon	— from the hostel to the top
on Mt Karáva of Agrapha	— from the public road to the top
on Mt Kithairón	— from Tsika locality to the top, and from the top to the Pétalo locality
on Mt Kirphy	— from Zemenó village to the top
on Mt Knimida	— from Kamména Voúrla village to Kariés village and to the top
on Mt Oíti	— from the Katavóthra locality to the top of Pýrgos
	— from Ypáti village to the hostel
on Mt Oxiá	— from Gardiki Omilaion village to the top
on Mt Parnassós	— from Yerontóvrahos peak to the Liákoura peak
	— from the Phterólakka ski centre to the Liákoura peak

on Mt Párnes	— from the Athen suburb of Thrakomakedónes to the hostel
	— from Paliohóri spring to the Skipiza spring and on to the Móla plateau.
	— from the hostel to the Skipiza spring
on Mt Pástra	— from Gáza locality to the top and on to the Óssios Meléttios monastery
on Mt Patéras	— from Paliokoúntoura village to the top
	— from Ághios Yeórgios village to the top
on Mt Voutsikáki of Ágrapha	— from Philakti village to the top
on Mt Yeránia	— from the Aërides saddle to the top

Thessaly:

on Hasia Mountain	— from Verdikoussia village to the top of the Mámali peak
On Mt Karava of Ágrapha	— from the Aghios Nikólaos saddle to the top
on Mt Kissavos	— from Spiliá village to the hostel and on to the top
	— from the Sinahóvrissi spring to the OTE telephone centre to the top, and on to the hostel
	— from Stómio village to the hostel
	— from Spiliá village to the villages of Hálkoma and Ambelákia and to the Vale of Temby
	— from Anatoli village to the locality of Livadákia to the OTE centre and on to the top
	— from Kallipéfki village to the villages of Paliá Skotina and Néa Skotina and on to the Metamórphosis peak
on Mt Olympos	— from Sparmós village to the Vrissopoúles hostel
	— from Kokkinoplós village to the Stalagmatiá locality, and on to the peaks of Christáki and Skolió.

Euboea:

on Mt Dirphi	— from the hostel to the top
on Mt Xerovoúni	— from the Dirphi hostel to the top

Crete:

on Mt Psiloritis	— from the Kamáres locality to that of Akólita

Rhodes:

on Mt Attávyros	— from Émpona village to the top

Epirus:

on Mt Smólikas	— from Samarina village to the top

Mountain camping in Peristéra village on Mt Helmós. (Photo J. Atamian)

on Mt Tzoumérka	— from Katarráktis village to the top of the Kataphidi peak

Macedonia:

on Mt Olympos	— from Priónia locality to the Spilios Agapitós hostel, and to the Mytikas peak
	— from the Diakládossi locality to the Petrós-trounga locality and on to the King Paul hostel.
	— from the Xeroláki locality to that of Lianoxiá and to the Yóssos Apostolidis hostel.
on Mt Pangaion	— from Avli village to Argýris Petaloúdas hostel
on Mt Piéria	— from the Áno Miliá hostel to the Pritsmantila locality and to that of Láka and on to the Pénde Pýrgoi peak
	— from the Áno Miliá hostel to the localities of Borlékkia, Kopánes, Toúphes, Avdélla and on to the top of Phlámbouro peak
on Mt Vourinos	— from the church of Ághios Penteleîmon to the top

GREEK MOUNTAINEERING AND WINTERSPORT CLUBS AND SOCIETIES

ASSOCIATE MEMBERS OF THE NATIONAL FEDERATION OF SKI AND ALPINISM (N.F.S.A.)
GAC = Greek Alpine Club

Name of Club	Address	Tel. from Athens (01)
GAC Aharnés (Menidi) Attika	Kentriki Plateia	01-2461.528
GAC Aighion	S. Lontou & Aratou	0691-25.285
GAC Amphikleia	Amphikleia Parnassidos	0234-22.640
GAC Aráchova	Arachova	0267-31.392
GAV Aspra Spitia	Paralia Distomou	0267-41.552
GAC Athens	Plateia Kapnikareas 2	·01-3231.867
GAC Dráma	Ephedron Axiomatikon 21	0521-23.054, 23.055
GAC Elefsina	Elefsina	01-5546.572
GAC Flórina	Tagmatarhou M. Pholledaki 33	0385-28.008
GAC Halkida	Tsirigoti 10	0221-25.230
GAC Haniá, (Crete)	Mihelidaki 5	0821-24.647
GAC Ioánnina	Monaimidou 6	0651-2.138
GAC Iráklion (Crete)	Dikaiosinis 53	081-287.110
GAC Karpenissi	Zinopoulou 25	0237-22.394. 23.051
GAC Kalavryta		0692-22.346
GAC Katerini	Vas. Konstantinou 8	0351-23.102
GAC Kavála	Mégaro Emborikou Epimelitiriou	051-21.238
GAC Kérkyra (Corfu)	Moustoxidou 11	0661-29.542
GAC Kozáni	H. Mouka 3	0461-25.600
GAC Lamia	Ypsilantou 25	0231-26.786
SKI CLUB Lamia	Ypsilantou 37	0231-23.696
GAC Lárissa	Vassilissis Sofias 15	011-220.097
GAC Litóhoro	Kentriki Plateia	0352-21.329
GAC Livadiá	Philonos 6	0261-29.232
GAC Métsovon	Nikolaou Gatsou 2	0656-41.249
GAC Náoussa	Plateia Truman	0332-28.567
GAC Pátra	Pantanassis 29	061-273.912
GAC Réthymno (Crete)	Arkadiou 143	0831-22.710
GAC Sérres	Merarhias 21	0321-23.724
GAC Spárta	Kentriki Plateia	0731-26.574, 26.444
GAC Thessaloniki	Karolou Dil 15	031-278.288
GAC Tripoli	Tripolis	071-222.101/102
GAC Vólos	Dimitriados 92	0421-25.696
GAC Xilókastro	Kentron Neolitos	—

INDEPENDENT WINTERSPORTS AND MOUNTAINEERING ASSOCIATIONS

Athens Skilovers' Club	Anagnostopoulou 8	01-3600.257
Greek Alpinists' Club of Athens	Pheidiou 18	01-3634.817

The GAC Náoussa hostel at Tría Pygádia on Mt Vérmion. (Photo GAC Náoussa)

Greek Alpinists' Club of Thessaloniki	Ionos Dragoumi 19	031-222.278
Mountaineering Club		222.238
of Thessaloniki	Mitropolitou Gennadiou 8	031-222.278, 222.234

EXCURSION CLUBS

Members of the Greek Federation of Excursion Clubs which have Mountaineering Sections

Nature Club of Piraeus	Alkividadou 143	01-4170.814
Athens Hiking Club	Kaningos 12	01-3622.938
Hiking Club of Piraeus	Aghiou Konstantinou 9	01-477.561
"O Pan"	Ioulianou 26, Athens	01-8224.777
Lamias Open Air Club	Nevropoleos 98	—
Association of the Greek Alpinists of Thessaloniki	Plateia Aristotélous 5	031-224.710
"Attikos"	Gladstonos 3, Athens	01-3616-747
Union of Mountaineers and Nature lovers	Mavrokordatou 7, Athens	01-3607 093 3606.924
Zinon Club of Piraeus	I. Dragatsi 2-4	01-470.810
Krystallis Club of Piraeus	G.A. Kountouriótou 145	01-474.094

WINTERSPORT CENTRES AND FACILITIES
IN THE GREEK MOUNTAINS

mountain	locality, height	managers	telephone	facilities
Vérmion	Mire-Lákka 1,570m	GAC Béroia	0332-412	Many skiruns with chair and anchor lifts, hostel with 60 beds
Vérmion	Tría Pygádia 1,450m	GAC Náoussa	—	Two hostels, with 60 and 35 beds, many ski runs, ski lifts
Veloúhi	Seïtáni- Piáto 1,840m	Karpenísi Ski Centre Ltd. and GAC Karpenísi	0237-22.002	Many skiruns with four ski lifts and "ratrak", hostel with 44 beds
Diphri	Liri 1,150m	GAC Halkída	0228-51.285	Small 240m skirun with one ski lift, hostel with 30 beds
Kissavos	Kánalos 1,604m	GAC Lárissa	—	Under construction
Ménnalon	Ostrakinas plateau, 1,540m	GAC Tripoli	0796-21.227	Hostel with 16 beds, two ski lifts
Pangaio	Hatzigeorgiou 1,750m	GAC Kavála	—	Small 350m ski lift, hostel with 10 beds
Parnassós	Phterólakka	National Tourist Organisation	—	Many ski runs, many chair lifts, hostel with 28 beds, restaurant, bar
Parnassós	Yerontó- vrahos 1,900m	Athens Ski Lover's Club	—	Many ski runs, two ski lifts, hostel
Pílion	Agriólefkes 1,350 m	GAC Vólos	0421-91.155	Hostel with 80 beds, another with 34 beds a little further down in Haniá. Many ski runs with various types of lifts

195

WINTERSPORT CENTRES AND FACILITIES
IN THE GREEK MOUNTAINS
(Continued)

Piéria	Pénde Pýrgoi 1,450m	GAC Katerini	—	Ski run with one ski lift under construction
Phalakró Drámas	Ághio Pnévma 1,800m	GAC Dráma	—	400m ski lift being expanded
Vitsi	Vigla Pisoderiou 1,650m	GAC Flórina	0385-22.354	Two ski lifts, hostel for 54-70
Ziria	Oropédio 1,650 m	—	—	Two with 50 and 20 beds. Facilities under construction
Mountains of Métsovon	—	GAC Métsovo	0656-41.249	Ski runs and one chair lift

The ski centre of the National Tourist Organization at Phterólakka locality on Mt Parnassós.

GREEK MOUNTAIN HOSTELS

mountain	locality	height	beds	managing club and hostel tel
Lefká Óri	Kallérgi	1,680 m	30	GAC Haniá, Crete
Lefká Óri (White Mountains)	Vólikas	1,480 m	40	GAC Haniá, Crete
Psiloritis	Prínos	1,100 m	16	GAC Iráklion, Crete
Taïgetos	Varvára	1,600 m	28	GAC Sparta
Parnon	Arnómousga	1,450 m	35	GAC Spárta
Panahaïkón	Psárthi	1,500 m	50	GAC Patras
Panahaïko	Prasoúdi	1,000 m	16	GAC Patras
Helmós	PoulioúVríssi	2,100 m	12	GAC Aighion
Ziria Á	Oropédio	1,650 m	50	NFSA
Ziria B	Pórtes	1,750 m	20	NFSA
Ménnalon	Ostrakinas plateau	1,540 m	20	GAC Tripoli
Párnes	Báphi	1,165 m	100	GAC Athens
Párnes	Varimbóppi	—	10	GAC Athens
Ohi	Kastanólongos	—	—	Municipality of Káristos
Díphri	Liri	1,100 m	36	GAC Halkida
Parnassós	Sarandári	1,900 m	28	GAC Athens
Vardoúsia	Pittimáliko	1,750 m	18	GAC Lamia
Vardoúsia	Pittimáliko	1,850 m	18	Athens Hiking Club
Veloúhi	Seïtáni	1,840 m	44	GAC Karpenísi
Oíti	Trápeza	1,800 m	28	GAC Lamia
Kallídromon	—	—	—	Lamia Open Air Club
Ghióna	Lákka Karvoúni	1,700 m	—	Athens Hiking Club
Oxiá	—	1,700 m	40	GAC Lamia

Mountain	Location	Elevation	Capacity	Club / Contact
Pílion	Agriólefkes	1,350 m	80	GAC Vólos, 0421-39.136
Pílion	Pilévs-Hánia	1,200 m	34	Drákeia municipality, 0421-39.155
Pílion	Hánia	1,200 m	40	O PAN, 0421-39.542
Pílion	Road to Agriólefkes	1,280 m	8	GAC Vólos
Kíssavos	Kánalos	1,600 m	40	GAC Lárissa
Kóziakas	—	—	—	Educational Excursion Club Trikala
Ólympos	Balkóni (Spílios Agapitós)	2,100 m	100	NFSA 0352-21.800
Ólympos	Vrissopoúles	1,900 m	50	Armed Forces, OTE station at Elassóna
Ólympos	Plateau of the Muses (King Paul)	2,650 m	18	GAC Katerini
Ólympos	Plateau of the Muses (Yióssos Apostolidis)	2,750 m	—	AGAT
Ólympos	Stavrós	1,000 m	30	GAC Thessaloniki
Piéria	Áno Miliá	1,000 m	40	GAC Katerini, 0351-21.284
Vérmio	Mire Láka	1,570 m	60	GAC Vérria
Vérmio	Xenónas Kato Vermiou	—	18	GAC Thessaloniki
Vérmio	Tría Pygádia	1,450 m	35	GAC Náoussa
Vítsi	Vígla Pisoderíou	1,600 m	60	GAC Flórina, 0385-22.354
Hortiátis	—	—	—	AGAT
Óri Vrontoús (Laï Liás)	—	1,500 m	25	GAC Sérres
Phalakrón Drámas	Bartiseva	1,142 m	16	GAC Dráma

Phlakrón Drámas	Horós	1,700 m	18	GAC Dráma
Phalakrón Drámas	Kouri	1,400 m	—	GAC Dráma
Pangaion	A. Petaloúdas hostel (Bláhika Kalívia)	1,550 m	25	GAC Kavála
Pangaion	S. Hatzigeorgiou hostel	1,750 m	10	GAC Kavála
Mitsikélli	—	1,400 m	25	GAC Ioánnina
Tsoúka Róssa *	Vakarátsa	1,450 m	—	GAC Ioánnina
Gamíla (Týmphi)	Astrákas saddle	1,950 m	28	GAC Ioánnina
Hortiátis	—	1,008 m	—	GAC Thessaloniki

* This is the mountain in the Pindus range, not to be confused with the other Tsoúka Rossa which is a peak of the Mt Gamila massif.

GAC = Greek Alpine Club
AGAT = Association of the Greek Alpinists of Thessaloniki
NFSA = National Federation of Ski and Alpinism

One of the Mt Helidóna peaks.

Above: Mountaineers on the saddle "Diásselotoú Kinigoú" on Mt Helmós, en route for the Styx valley. *Below:* The author (left) with fellow mountaineers, outside the meteorological station on the Aghios Antónis peak of Mt Olympos.

At the Phterólakka ski centre on Mt Parnassós.

BIBLIOGRAPHY

Apanta	K, Krystállys
Die mythologie der Griechen (Greek edision)	K. Kerényi
Enimerotiko deltio (Information bulletin)	GAC Athens
Helliniká dimotiká tragoúdia (Greek popular songs)	M. Peránthis
History of Modern Greece (in Greek)	T. Vournás
History of the Greek Revolution (Greek edision)	G. Finley
I hellinki epanástasis (The Greek Revolution)	D. Kókkinos
I laïki téhni tou Piliou (The popular art of Mt Pilio)	K. Makris
I physis (Nature)	Hellenic Society for the Protection of Nature
Istoria tis katohis (History of the occupation)	D. Gatópoulos
La résistance greque — 1940-44 (Greek edition)	A. Kédros
Magazine "Ekdromika"	Kl. Dendrinós
Magazine "Orivasia" (Mountain Climbing)	Greek Alpinists Club of Athens
Magazine "To Vounó" (The Mountain)	N.F.S.A
Moraïtika tragoúdia (songs of the Peloponnese)	G. Tarsouli
O Attikós	Attikós-Excursions Club
Olympos	E. Eleftheriádis
Olympos	I. Nikópoulos